KFK KINGFISHER KNOWLEDGE

COMMUNICATION
FROM HIEROGLYPHS TO HYPERLINKS

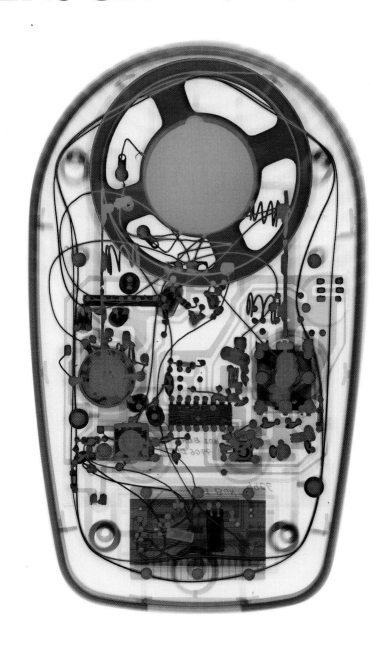

iuda. Sorte domini eledionis vincere...
compleretur: sicq3 paulus commes...
dicam apostolicis adibz dare. que illi...
cetera stimulū recalcitrare. que dili...
ret. Quod et legentibz ac requirentibz...
deū. et si per singula repediri a nobis...
utile fuerat: sciens tamē q3 operantem...
agricolā oportet de suis fructibus...
dere. vitauim° publicā curiositatem et...
ne nō tā volentibz deū demōstrare vide...
retur. quā fastidientibus prodidisse...
Explicit prefacio. Incipit euangeliū...
secundum lucā. Prohemium ipi...
beati luce in euangelium ipi...

Quoniam quidem multi co-
nati sūt ordinare nar:
ratōnes qi i nobis com-
plete sūt reꝛ. sicut tradi
derūt nobis q ab initio
ipi viderūt. et ministri
fuerūt sermonis: visū ē et michi assecuto
oīnia a priꝛcipio diligēter eꝛ ordie tibi
scribere optie theophile: ut cognoscas
eoꝛ verboꝛ de qbz eruditꝰ es veritatē.]-
Vit in diebus herodis re
gis iudee sacerdos quidam
nomine zacharias de vi

COMMUNICATION
FROM HIEROGLYPHS TO HYPERLINKS

Richard Platt

Foreword by
Lord MacLaurin

KINGFISHER

KINGFISHER

First published 2004 by Kingfisher

This edition printed 2008 by Kingfisher
an imprint of Macmillan Children's Books
a division of Macmillan Publishers Limited
The Macmillan Building, 4 Crinan Street, London N1 9XW
Basingstoke and Oxford
Associated companies throughout the world
www.panmacmillan.com

ISBN 978-0-7534-0956-5

Copyright © Macmillan Children's Books 2004

9 8 7 6 5 4 3 2 1
BCA/0408/TWP/MA(MA)/130GRYMA/F

A CIP catalogue record for this book is available from the British Library.

Printed in Singapore

GO FURTHER...
INFORMATION PANEL KEY:

 websites and further reading

 career paths

 places to visit

◄ Thomas Edison (1847–1931) set up kinetoscope arcades where people could watch short film clips at the rows of coin-operated machines.

Contents

Foreword

There are hundreds of different ways to share your feelings and thoughts with others, and this book is all about how communication is possible.

When I was asked to write this foreword, I started wondering about the historical developments in the methods of communication. If you think about it, for centuries we humans used speech as our main form of communication, and not much else. Native Americans developed a method of sending messages by smoke signals, and other people sent messages by beating rhythms on drums, but for thousands of years, there were few changes in the ways people shared information with each other.

When the written word came along, it meant that we could deliver messages in various ways: trained birds and messengers on foot or on horseback carried and delivered letters. In the last hundred years, things have really taken off and we have seen hundreds of amazing inventions. The big change probably started when we developed a proper postal system using mail coaches. These ensured a relatively cheap and reliable way to send a letter from A to B. Then there was the telegraph system and eventually the telephone – and this really did change people's lives.

In the 20th century, there have been even more amazing developments – firstly, the radio, and then in the 1950s, the television arrived in our sitting rooms. It was without a doubt one of the most remarkable inventions of our lifetime: suddenly we could have pictures from all over the world in our own homes – sometimes as they were happening!

The last two decades have been the most remarkable in terms of the development of communications technologies. In the late 1980s, we had not heard of the internet, now we use it daily as a work tool and a major source of information and entertainment. Another remarkable invention was the mobile telephone. I am chairman of Vodafone, one of the world's largest communications organizations. Around the time of the invention of the internet, Vodafone was a small company based in Newbury, England. Now we are global. Then, mobile telephones were novelty items and were about the size (and weight) of a large brick, whereas now they are considered a necessity and can fit easily into your pocket.

While you are reading this book, spare a thought for people who have problems communicating. Imagine if you could not speak, or found communicating with others a very difficult experience, or if you could not express how you feel. I support an extremely worthwhile charity called ICAN. This charity helps children with communication difficulties learn to overcome them. An inability to communicate can be the difference between success and failure at school, and hardships in later life. It can mean the difference between being a happy child and a very unhappy one.

This book is called *Communication: from Hieroglyphs to Hyperlinks* – hieroglyphs were a mystery until someone stumbled upon the Rosetta Stone, and until recently I would not have been able to tell you what a hyperlink was! Reading this book was a terrific learning experience for me – I hope that you enjoy it as much as I did.

Lord MacLaurin of Knebworth – Chairman, Vodafone Group Plc, and patron of ICAN

CHAPTER 1

Face to face

What is communication? It is a letter, a text, shouting, waving, and nodding. Do not forget television, radio, books and newspapers. The list is long: much longer than you might imagine. For people are not the only ones that communicate. Long before humans walked the earth, animals had solved the problem of communication. They used sound, colour, taste, smell and movement to send messages to each other.

We may think of speech as our simplest communications skill, but the very first humans could not talk. Instead, they grunted and used gestures. Even when people learned to speak, they never lost these basic, 'no-words' communications skills. Next time you have a face-to-face conversation, tune in to your animal side. You may express yourself better by punctuating your sentences with facial expressions and body language.

Just as speech began with grunts, pictures marked the dawn of written communication. Daubed on cave walls or pressed in mud, they made a lasting record of messages. Picture writing is still used to break through language barriers: in a foreign city there is no mistaking the 'paper-doll' figure on a toilet door.

Animal communication

Barking, buzzing, singing and wagging, animals are far from dumb. They may not be able to talk using words and sentences, but they never stop chattering. Instead, they rely on scent, sound, light, colour and movement for signalling. They use messages to warn of danger, to lead their friends to food, for flirting with their mates, and for much, much more. In fact, communication in the animal world is so rich and varied that it makes humans look like the silent ones. We rely mostly on our ears and eyes to communicate with each other, and although animals have powerful senses of hearing and sight, they can also use smell and touch to send signals.

▲ By 'dancing' in a figure-of-eight pattern, a bee can tell fellow bees in the hive exactly where to find a rich source of food. The angle of the dance shows the direction of the food and the quicker the dance, the closer the food.

Calling and crying

Animals use sound for signalling because sound travels long distances, and it can also work by day or by night. However, sound fades very quickly, so it does not help hungry predators to track and eat calling animals. It is also an adaptable way of signalling. By changing the volume, speed and pitch, it is possible to make a huge variety of calls.

When a songbird spots a skulking cat, it sings a special 'look out!' chirp that sends the other small birds zooming to safety. These warning songs are so special that even humans can hear and recognize them. However, many other animal sound signals are in a form that we cannot understand – or hear. For example, giant finback whales send messages with a sound that is too low in pitch for our ears to detect. And, at the other end of the musical scale, the squeaks made by bats are too high for us to hear.

▼ Humpback whales communicate with their mates in haunting 'songs'. The sequence of moans, chirps, cries, ratchets and snores, is very loud and has been heard by sailors through the wooden hulls of ships. It sounds so strange that at least one crew has left their ship, convinced that it was haunted.

Apes use their expressive faces to communicate with each other. Some of their expressions look eerily like our own smiles and frowns, but their grimaces often have quite different meanings from ours. For example, a chimp's bare-toothed smile is a warning, not a greeting. Less advanced animals also use visual signals: think of a dog's wagging tail.

There are some animals that do not stop at movement and actually change colour to send messages. For instance, the throat of the male stickleback – a spiny-finned fish – turns redder when he is cross, and when he wants to attract a female. Tiny fire-flies communicate in a similar way: they flash like lighthouses to signal that they are looking for hot dates.

▼ Chimpanzees are great communicators, using sound, gestures and expressions to chat in their African rainforest home. Captive chimps have learned to talk to people, by signing as deaf people do, or by pointing to pictures on a special keyboard.

Smelling and sniffing

Chemical communication – scents and tastes – does a very different job for animals. Unlike sounds, scents linger, so they are a useful way for mammals to leave marks that say 'I live here – keep out'. Insects that live in groups, such as ants, have a rich 'language' of smells. They make scents to signal danger, to lay trails for others to follow, and to persuade fellow ants to groom them or carry them to safety when danger threatens.

Grinning and blushing

When they are close together, many animals use visual signals to send messages to each other.

Without words

Long before humans learned how to speak, they were using their hands and faces to express themselves and to pass on knowledge. Today we still rely on expressions and gestures to communicate our ideas to others. When we are talking, we grin and frown, raise our eyebrows, and stab at the air with fists and fingers to make a point. Even the way we sit can tell a different story from our words, revealing whether we are lying or telling the truth.

▶ We will never know how hominids used expressions and gestures to communicate before they learned to speak. Studies of chimps – our nearest non-human relatives – have not helped. Though many scientists have investigated chimp communication, no one understands more than a few words of 'chimp-ese'.

send signals with our posture (the position of our body, arms and legs). It is not too difficult to guess what others are thinking by studying their body language. For example, folding your arms during a discussion or an argument makes a barrier that means 'I do not agree' or 'I am not listening to you'. If someone touches or hides their mouth while they are talking, it often means that they are not telling the truth. Leaning back, with your hands behind your head, suggests 'I am smarter than you', but

may not be lying, he may just have cut himself shaving.

Hand signals

Next time you have an argument, try sitting on your hands. You will be surprised how much you miss them. Although we use our hands all the time when we talk, not all of the gestures we use mean something. Some – like pounding the table – just make our words seem more important, but other gestures help us to explain what we are saying. Pointing, for example, helps to make it clear who or what we are talking about, and a clenched fist often shows anger more clearly than words ever could.

▲ Some gestures, such as thumbs-up for 'OK', mean the same everywhere. Long ago, a pointing finger to show travellers where to go was carved on road-signs, but in an argument, it accuses the person it is pointed at.

▼ Although shouting does not always win an argument, the loudness of our speech can help to emphasize (stress) what we are saying. On the other hand, speaking quietly encourages the person listening to lean forward and pay careful attention to what we are saying.

▶ 800,000-year-old skulls dug up in Java, Indonesia, have bulges above the part of the brain that controls speech. This suggests they are the remains of people who could talk. These people also made long sea journeys which would have been difficult to organize if they could not speak.

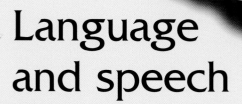

Language and speech

Speech is one of the most adaptable and powerful ways of communicating. We can shout a quick warning without a moment's hesitation. Yet with thought, preparation and care, we can use speech to explain complex and difficult ideas. We can even 'talk people round' to our point of view. However, learning to speak is not easy – our distant ancestors never managed it – and most of us celebrate our first birthday before we say our first word.

▼ Stephen Hawking (b.1942) is handicapped by motor neurone disease (MND), an illness that can affect all our muscles, including those of the throat that we use to speak. Although MND took away his ability to talk, Hawking has become one of the world's greatest physicists. He uses a computer with a special speech synthesizer to explain and dictate his brilliant ideas.

When humans began to speak

If fossils preserved words as well as they preserve the bones of our ancestors, we would know exactly when humans first learned to speak. Unfortunately they do not, and the scientists and archaeologists who dig up ancient skeletons from the ground have found few clues as to how these early people communicated with each other.

It is not surprising that scientists disagree about when humans first learned to speak. Although some think the ability to talk is about 800,000 years old, there are other scientists who believe we were all dumb until about 300,000 years ago.

Skulls and sailing boats

Those scientists who choose the more recent date of the two, use the small skulls of ancient people as their evidence. They argue that the brains of our oldest ancestors were tiny, and that they simply did not have the 'brain power' to learn to talk. Skull shapes also show the position of the larynx (the voice-box in the throat that enables us to form words). If it is situated too high in the throat, the ability to speak is impossible. However, what these ancient people *did* tells quite a different story. About 800,000 years ago some of them crossed wide oceans – how could they build and sail ships without talking to each other?

Learning to speak

We learn to talk by listening to others and imitating them. Although most babies understand a few words by the time they are a year old, talking only comes a few months later. This is because they need to practise controlling the speaking equipment in their mouths (such as the tongue) and the equipment in their throats (such as the larynx). Most babies say their first words between 12 and 18 months, and can make simple sentences of three or more words by the time they are two.

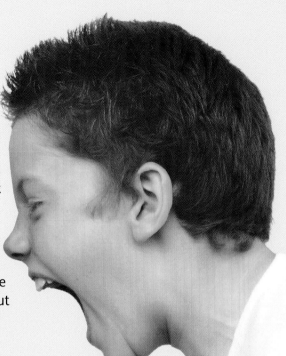

What is surprising about learning to speak is that we have only one chance at it. Scientists believe that if we have not mastered speech by the time we are teenagers, we will never really manage it. Raising a child in silence to prove this would be a cruel experiment. However, there are children who have been brought up by animals and did not hear speech when they were young. Those children who first met other humans after the age of twelve rarely learned to say more than a few words.

Speech therapy

Very few people have had to suffer in this way. However, there are as many as one in ten humans who have difficulty communicating through speech. Most of these people have lost the ability to speak through an accident or illness. Fortunately, speech therapists can often help to improve or sometimes even restore their speech. Where therapists fail to do this, patients are fitted with speech synthesizers and other aids – giving them back their lost voices.

◄ 'Wolf children' are children who cannot talk because they have never heard speech to imitate. Some wolf children have been raised by animals, though not always wolves, and others had parents who never spoke to them. Such handicaps are rare, and fewer than 50 wolf children have been found since 1900.

▲ Cave paintings, such as this example from the Cave of the Arrows in Mexico, most often show the animals that hunters of the time wanted to catch. Although humans appear in this painting, they are rare in the world's oldest cave paintings found in southern Europe.

Writing it down

Talking is a quick way to tell someone what you are thinking, but the message is gone as soon as the echoes of your words die away. To make your communications last, you need to record them – by carving, scratching, painting, pressing or printing. Written messages began on cave walls, with Stone Age pictures of prancing antelope and fearsome mammoths. In Asia, Africa and the Americas, scribes (writing experts) made these rough drawings into written languages. They used the new writing to record their stories, their history – and receipts for beer!

Painting cave walls

Prehistoric people started painting on the walls of caves 30,000 years ago. They used charcoal, mud and sometimes even their own blood to create vivid scenes of animals and hunters. Often the painters clambered far below the ground to paint pictures in places that few people visited. It is hard to tell why these pictures were made. Archaeologists cannot agree whether the paintings were just for decoration, or if they had a magic, lucky meaning. But whatever their use, these cave paintings mark the start of written communication.

Earliest known writing

The next big step forward was the invention of writing in Sumer (modern-day Iraq). In 3300BCE the Sumerians began scratching and pressing messages into flat lumps of soft clay. At first they used tiny pictures to represent different objects and ideas. But gradually these pictures looked less and less like the objects they represented. Eventually Sumerian scribes gave up drawing these intricate pictures and turned their marks into standard signs, with each sign standing for a whole word. The scribes used the wedge-shaped end of a cut reed as a stylus (writing tool), and created a kind of writing known as cuneiform. The writing was so successful that the Sumerians' neighbours also began to use it.

▼ Scribes of Sumer pressed the world's oldest adventure story into soft clay some 4,000 years ago. In the story, the hero Gilgamesh (below) attacks a fire-breathing monster whose gaze turns men to stone. The cuneiform writing that scribes used forms the background to this page.

Many of the clay tablets the Sumerians created still exist. Although some are business records, such as beer receipts, the Sumerians also used cuneiform to write down the world's first superhero story – the epic of Gilgamesh.

Picture-writing improved

Outside Sumer, scribes found other ways to adapt and improve pictures so that they could record language. In Egypt, the pictures were more simple. They also used a few pictures to stand for some of the sounds of speech, just as we use letters today. The result was hieroglyphic writing which the Egyptian scribes began to use 5,000 years ago. Within three centuries the Egyptians had devised quicker ways of writing, but they kept hieroglyphics for important and special messages until about CE400.

Elsewhere in the world, picture-writing thrived. When Spanish adventurers travelled to Central America in the 16th century CE, they discovered that the Aztec people who ruled Mexico also used pictures for writing. Their written language looked a little like the Egyptians' hieroglyphics, although the two kinds of writing developed 3,500 years and 12,000km apart.

Modern picture-writing

In some Asian countries, such as Japan and China, people still write using small pictures. Many pictures stand for a whole word, and there have to be many signs to represent every object or idea. Writing in Chinese, for example, involves learning about 4,000 pictures. Most of the pictures have been simplified so that they are quicker to write, making their meaning hard to guess from the sign. Some are easy to recognize, such as the Japanese sign that looks like an open umbrella – and means exactly that.

► Aztec priests used picture-writing like this to record Mexico's history, details of temple ceremonies and tax demands. Although the Aztecs' written language had few words, this did not matter: priests used the writing like notes, filling in the details from memory.

SUMMARY OF CHAPTER 1: FACE TO FACE

The dawn of communication

Communication began long before human beings walked the earth. Animals used sound, movement, colour change, scent and taste to send messages to each other. Our ape ancestors became expert communicators, and when humans evolved from them, we developed their communication skills further. At first, humans could not speak, but used the apes' sounds, expressions and gestures to get the message across. We still use these grimaces to emphasize our words. We smile and frown, or raise our eyebrows to express surprise and we wave our hands when we are excited. We also send subtle signals about our mood, using our arms, legs and bodies.

People probably learned to talk more than 300,000 years ago. Experts cannot agree about the exact date, but, judging by what people achieved in the distant past, they were communicating effectively much earlier than this. However, the evidence of fossilized skulls suggests that we learned to speak more recently.

Learning to talk

Children learn to speak by listening to adults and imitating what they hear. Few babies talk much before their first birthday. Even after their first words, learning to form complete sentences is a slow process. Children raised in silence rarely learn to speak fluently, and even if they hear speech later in life, they often find it impossible to learn more than a few words.

Though talking is a quick way to communicate, words do not last, and people began making permanent records some 30,000 years ago. They started by painting images on cave walls. These showed the animals they hunted and, occasionally, human figures. The first writing used pictures too, although they were smaller and simpler than cave paintings. Writing began around 5,000 years ago, when the Sumerians used cut reeds to scratch and press pictures into damp clay. The people of Egypt carved and painted a form of picture-writing that we call hieroglyphics.

Other people around the world also developed their own picture-writing systems and, today, Chinese and Japanese characters are still based on pictures.

Go further...

Listen to animal sounds:
www.animal-sounds.org

Write your name in hieroglyphs:
www.upennmuseum.com/
hieroglyphsreal.cgi

Learn how British charity ICAN is helping children to communicate:
www.ican.org.uk

How Animals Communicate by Bobbie Kalman (Crabtree Publishing Co, 1996)

Decoding Egyptian Hieroglyphs: How to Read the Secret Language of the Pharaohs by Bridget McDermott (Chronicle, 2001)

Anthropologist
Although anthropologists study human origins and culture, some specialize in primate communications.

Archaeologist
Studies peoples and cultures from history using inscriptions and wall paintings.

Historical linguist
Investigates languages used in the past, including the understanding and translation of non-alphabetic writing systems.

Speech therapist
Helps those suffering from speech impediments, such as stammers, to communicate more effectively.

See hieroglyphics and the Rosetta stone, the key to understanding them at The British Museum, Great Russell Street, London WC1B 3DG.
Telephone: +44 (0) 20 7323 8299
www.thebritishmuseum.ac.uk

Hear dolphins communicating in Scotland's Moray Firth at North Kessock Seal and Dolphin Centre.
Telephone: +44 (0) 1463 731866

Visit a cave in France containing some of the world's most famous wall paintings:
Lascaux Cave, Montignac, Dordogne, France.
Telephone: +33 (0) 5 53 35 50 10
www.culture.gouv.fr:80/culture/
arcnat/lascaux/en/index3.html

CHAPTER 2

From me to you

For a long time, communications were strictly person–to–person. If you wanted to send a letter, a messenger had to carry it for you. Postal services made things simpler, but not much quicker, as the letter still had to travel by horse-drawn carriage to its final destination.

Flashing signals or flapping flags were faster than horses, but hilltop beacons can say little more than 'yes' or 'no', and even the best visual signal travels only as far as the eye can see.

The discovery of electricity changed this. Telegraph wires buzzed, not with speech, but with pulses of power. Soon, telephone calls replaced this code of 'dots and dashes'. In at least one way, these calls are like the written messages of the past: they are still me-to-you signals. And nothing brings people closer than a one-to-one, personal message.

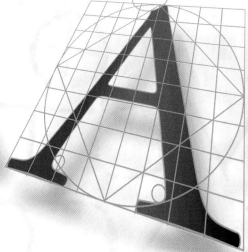

▶ As people adapted the alphabet to suit their own language, they changed the letters a little. Here is the letter 'A' written in Semitic script, ancient Greek, and our own Roman alphabet. The green grid shows how circles and straight lines create the letter's shape.

Alphabets

Once we have the knack of reading and writing, nothing seems simpler. No wonder we say things are 'as easy as A-B-C'. However, inventing the alphabet was not at all simple. The change from picture-writing systems to the letters that we use today began some 3,000 years ago. Our alphabet was not finished until the 11th century CE, when scribes added 'W' to complete the Roman alphabet's 26 letters.

◀ Although the Arabic alphabet also developed from the Semitic and, like ours, has 26 letters, the shape of the letters changes according to whether they occur at the start, the middle or the end of the word.

Why not just use pictures?
The advantages of an alphabet over a picture-writing system seem obvious to us. Pictures stand for words or ideas, so writers need to learn hundreds of them before they can write. But in an alphabet, each letter stands for a single sound. In English, with 26 letters, it is possible to write anything we can say out loud. However, when picture-writing was the *only* way of writing, nobody noticed its drawbacks.

What, no vowels?
The first people to write using letters were probably the Phoenicians, who lived on the eastern coast of the Mediterranean Sea. In the 11th century BCE, they began to write what we now call Semitic script. Although their alphabet had 22 letters, it lacked the vowels 'A', 'E', 'I', 'O' and 'U'.

Borrowing the alphabet
The Phoenicians were a great seafaring nation, and it may have been their mariners who took the Semitic alphabet to Greece. The Greeks quickly grasped its advantages and adapted it to suit their own language. The Semitic alphabet had more consonants than the Greek alphabet, so the Greeks had consonants to spare.

They used these left over consonants to stand for vowel sounds, and created the first full alphabet between 1000 and 900BCE. Greek letters also gave the alphabet its name: the word is made by linking the first letter of the Greek alphabet, 'alpha' and the second letter, 'beta'.

The Roman alphabet

Just as the Greeks borrowed letters from the Phoenicians to write their own language, so the Etruscan people of Italy borrowed from the Greeks. They began using an alphabet in the 8th century BCE. The people of Rome used and improved the Etruscan alphabet. They used the letters 'A',' B', 'E', 'H', 'I', 'K', 'M', 'N', 'O', 'T', 'X' and 'Z' exactly as the Greeks had done. The Romans also adapted other Greek letters to have 'C', 'D', 'G', 'L', 'P', 'R', 'S' and 'Y'. The letters 'F', 'V' and 'Q' were no longer used in Greek, but the Romans polished them up and put them to work again. This gave us most of the letters we use today to write English.

Adding the finishing touches

The English alphabet has 26 letters, but the Roman had only 23. European scribes added 'J', 'U' and 'W' between the 6th and 11th centuries CE. Even as recently as the 19th century, some books still used 'I' and 'J' interchangeably. Although we can trace the roots of our alphabet back some 3,000 years, it was perfected less than two centuries ago.

The way the Roman alphabet is written has also changed. The Romans started with just capital letters. Writing developed slowly from these capitals. Roman writers adapted the capital letters a little to make them easier to read. However, by the 8th century CE, monks copying bibles and other religious books had devised a completely new way of writing, called 'minuscule'. Over the centuries that followed, this flowing, curving handwriting style became the small letters we use today.

▲ We write English from left to right, but Arabic writing goes from right to left. Some Asian languages go up and down the page, and this Greek writing, from 450BCE, even changes direction every other line!

▼ Romans often wrote on wooden boards coated in wax. Although the wax has long gone from the boards that have survived, it is still possible to read some of the letters where a heavy hand pressed them through to the wood.

► Marco Polo visited China when it was ruled by the Mongols. They were famed for their horse-riding ability, and today people from Mongolia keep alive the traditions of the mounted messengers that fascinated Marco Polo.

▼ Troops in World War II (1939–45) used pigeons to send messages from areas of intense fighting to distant control centres. The birds flew through fog, smoke, bullets and dust, delivering information when all other methods failed.

Messengers

More than 2,500 years ago Phidippides, history's most famous messenger, ran 40km with the news of a Greek victory at the Battle of Marathon. It is not surprising that, after delivering the message, he died from exhaustion! In the centuries that followed, few messengers have been quite as dedicated. The information they carried, though, was just as urgent. For until postal services began, servants took important messages personally, travelling on foot or on horseback to deliver news.

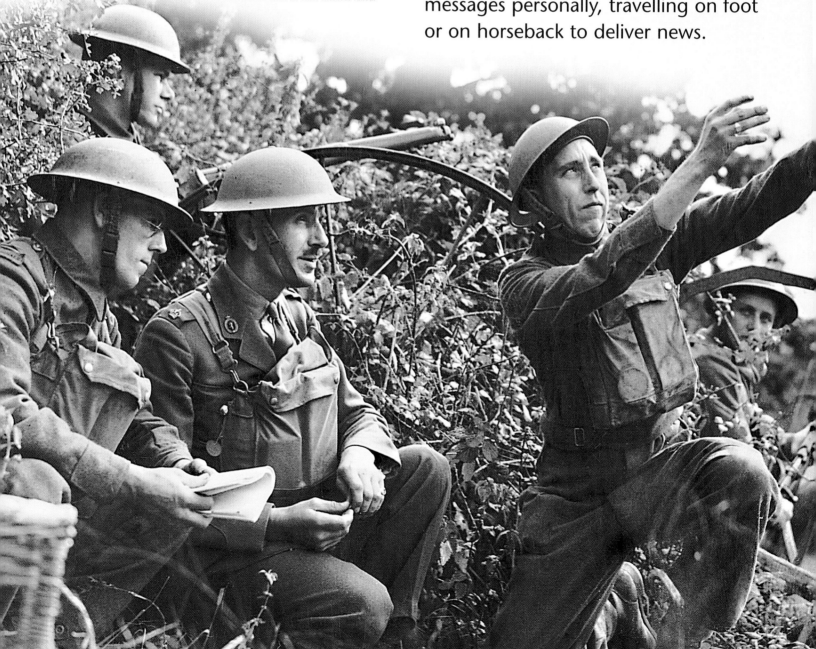

Riders and runners

Official messenger services began in the great empires of the past. Government messengers hurried to deliver urgent news in Egypt 4,000 years ago, and ten centuries later in China.

The Chinese messengers still ran an efficient service when the Venetian traveller, Marco Polo (1254–1324), visited the country in the 13th century. He reported that a relay of horse-back messengers carried urgent news up to 400km in a day.

Chinese runners also carried messages, each racing 5km at a time. Small bells fixed to their belts warned of their arrival, so that the next runner in the relay could be ready to snatch the letter and race onwards. Besides the letters, the runners also brought the emperor ripe fruit from the warmest parts of China.

Roman messengers

The rulers of ancient Rome also needed a messenger service to control their vast empire, which was spread over most of Europe and beyond. Their *cursus publicus* (state runners service) used a series of rest-houses spaced 12km apart on the main roads. During brief stops, messengers would swap their exhausted horses for rested ones, before galloping away with the mail.

In the 5th century CE, the Roman empire collapsed and the well-made roads broke up into muddy trails. Many of Europe's smaller countries did not need the messenger service of a mighty empire and eventually, the *cursus publicus* ceased to run.

Guilds and merchants

With the rise of guilds (business companies) in the 13th century, messengers were once again in demand. They carried letters for wealthy merchants in Italy. Similar messenger services began in Britain, France and other European countries. Not only did the messengers take information and news between the many great fairs where merchants gathered, but they also went farther afield, to places such as Constantinople (modern-day Istanbul) and Persia (modern-day Iran).

Airmail with a beak

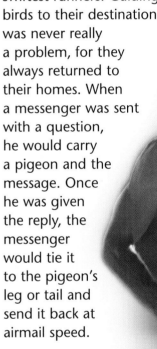

Messages were not always delivered by humans. Since the time of Egyptian pharaoh Rameses III (1198–1167BCE), pigeons have carried messages much faster than the swiftest runners. Guiding the birds to their destination was never really a problem, for they always returned to their homes. When a messenger was sent with a question, he would carry a pigeon and the message. Once he was given the reply, the messenger would tie it to the pigeon's leg or tail and send it back at airmail speed.

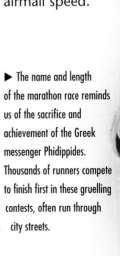

▶ The name and length of the marathon race reminds us of the sacrifice and achievement of the Greek messenger Phidippides. Thousands of runners compete to finish first in these gruelling contests, often run through city streets.

▲ Ever wondered what happens to your letter once you put it in the postbox? From the postbox, your letter is collected and transported by lorry to a sorting office.

▼ Mail-coaches travelled at double the speed of the post-boys they replaced: zooming along at an alarming 17km/h. Their journeys were not always smooth: bad roads delayed them, and armed highwaymen stopped the coaches and stole the mail.

◄ At the sorting office, machines cancel the stamps and sort mail by destination regions.
▲ Most inland mail is taken to the local sorting office by lorry, but airmail is shifted by aircraft to the destination country.

The postal service

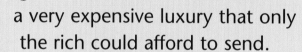

Posting a letter is so easy and familiar to us that we rarely think about what an amazing service we are using. The post office delivers our mail to anywhere in the country or world, it usually arrives within a few days, and the cost is relatively inexpensive – no matter how far the letter travels. However, it was not always this easy or this cheap. When postal services began in England and France, letters were a very expensive luxury that only the rich could afford to send.

▲ Famous riders of the Wild West worked for the Pony Express service. Calamity Jane (Martha Jane Cannary, 1852–1903) rode for the company, and Buffalo Bill (William Cody, 1846–1914) was just 15 when he delivered mail.

▲ Once airmail has reached its destination country, it is sorted by post office workers into regions or postcodes.

▲ From here, mail is taken to the local sorting office for that region, where it is sorted by street address. Inland mail would also be transported to local offices.

▲ Postmen then collect their mail from the sorting office.

▲ All mail is then hand delivered to postboxes.

First post

The first postal service was started in 1464 by King Louis XI of France. In Britain, 50 years later, the king set up a service for royal letters. The horse-riding post-boys were not meant to deliver letters for anyone else, but they did, and in 1581, an official public postal service began.

The post-boys were slow and often drank too much, and at the end of the 18th century, fast mail coaches replaced them. The coaches sped along, stopping at post-houses to change horses. Posting a letter was a costly business. Delivery was charged by distance: sending a letter 13km cost a labourer a whole day's wages.

American letters

Most of the American colonies (modern-day USA) had postal services by 1700, but as settlers spread out west across the continent, delivery times became longer and longer. Special high-speed services aimed to change this. The best known was the Pony Express, which linked Missouri and California.

Despite its fame, the company never made money, and within 18 months the electric telegraph (see page 26) put the riders out of work.

Penny post

Modern 'one-price' postal services began in England in 1837. Rowland Hill (1795–1879) showed that delivering a letter around the corner cost the post office almost as much as sending it the length of the country. He suggested a single price for letters of one penny to be paid by buying a stamp. Before this, the average price was six times higher, and the person receiving the letter had to pay the postman on delivery.

Hill's 'penny post' was a great success and the number of letters posted quickly paid for the cut-price service. Many other countries copied it too, starting with Switzerland and Brazil.

Posting letters abroad remained a problem until an international postal treaty in 1878. After this, sending a letter across the world needed a single stamp, no matter how many countries it passed through.

▶ Street postboxes were not an immediate success: people posted filth through the slots and often mice crept inside boxes and gnawed mail.

Flags and fires

A blazing beacon or a smoky fire may not seem the most obvious way to communicate, but when you just want to say 'yes' or 'no', these flaming signals are the quickest way to spread the news. They are also instantly visible from far away, so people have used them to send messages over long distances since ancient times. Fire carries only simple information, but there are other visual signals that are more versatile.

Flags, for example, can spell out whole sentences to those who understand their colourful code, and the reflection of mirrors can be used to send sentences over great distances.

◀ Just one or two flags are enough to send signals — as long as the person who is receiving the message can clearly see the position of the flags. Wig-wag signalling uses a single flag and semaphore signalling uses two. This sailor is signalling the letter 'E' in semaphore.

▶ By holding a blanket over a smoking fire, then lifting it, native Americans created signals from puffs of smoke. A single puff meant 'attention!' while three puffs in a row was the signal for danger.

Speedy beacons

A signal can easily speed along a chain of beacons in the time it takes to light a fire, and the higher a beacon is, the farther away it can be seen. Over 3,200 years ago, the Greeks built beacons to send signals from the city of Troy to their capital Mycenae, a great distance away. The flame of one beacon at the top of a 2,000m-high mountain could be seen 180km away.

Fire and smoke

Native Americans improved on existing flame communications so that they could use smoky fires to send more than just simple 'yes' and 'no' signals. By changing the number of fires and the spacing between them, they signalled their safe arrival at the end of a journey, an emergency, or how many enemies a war party had killed.

Shining mirrors

In the 19th century, there was conflict over land between native Americans and white Americans.

▶ Today, many naval ships keep signal flags for decoration. But in the days of sailing ships, using different-coloured flags was the only way to send a message to a vessel that was too far away to shout to. In this example, the red flag with the yellow cross stands for the letter 'R'.

United States army general, Nelson Miles (1835–1925), sent to Arizona to defeat the native Americans, quickly saw the value of visual signals in the clear desert air. Reflecting sunlight from mirrors, his men sent brilliant flashes to observers up to 50km away. By using the dots and dashes of Morse code (see page 26), they could easily transmit a 16-word message in one minute.

Flapping a message

The Greeks were using flags to send messages 2,400 years ago. However, flags were not used for advanced signalling until the 18th century, when the French navy devised a cunning flag code. This gave the 1,000 most common messages numbers. Different flags represented the numbers 0 to 9, so hoisting three flags to the masthead of a ship could quickly send a signal to the whole fleet. Other navies improved the scheme with flags representing each letter. For example, the English flag code 'AS' meant 'my ship has struck the rocks and is breaking up'.

◀ Claude Chappe's telegraph network carried messages all over France. Towers were spaced approximately 10km apart and two signallers worked in each tower. One signaller watched the neighbouring tower through a telescope and called out the signals to his partner. The partner would then waggle the arms on the roof, sending the message to the next tower.

Claude's telegraph

One of the cleverest methods of visual signalling was a French invention by Abbot Claude Chappe (1763–1805). He suggested building a network of towers, each with a movable H-shaped signal on top. Controls inside the tower adjusted the angles of the 'legs' and 'crossbar' of the H in a code that stood for letters of the alphabet. Each tower was in sight of two others: signallers inside watched their neighbours, and copied the messages. With this 'pass-it-on' system, messages could travel 115km in one minute.

Electric telegraph

In 1860, an urgent message took ten days to cross the United States in the saddlebags of a galloping pony. The following year, the same message took just minutes to arrive. For in 1861, telegraph wires linked the United States' east and west coasts for the first time. The wires crackled not with speech, but with long and short pulses of electrical power. This code of dots and dashes was named after Samuel Morse (1791–1872), the US artist who had helped perfect the electric telegraph 25 years earlier.

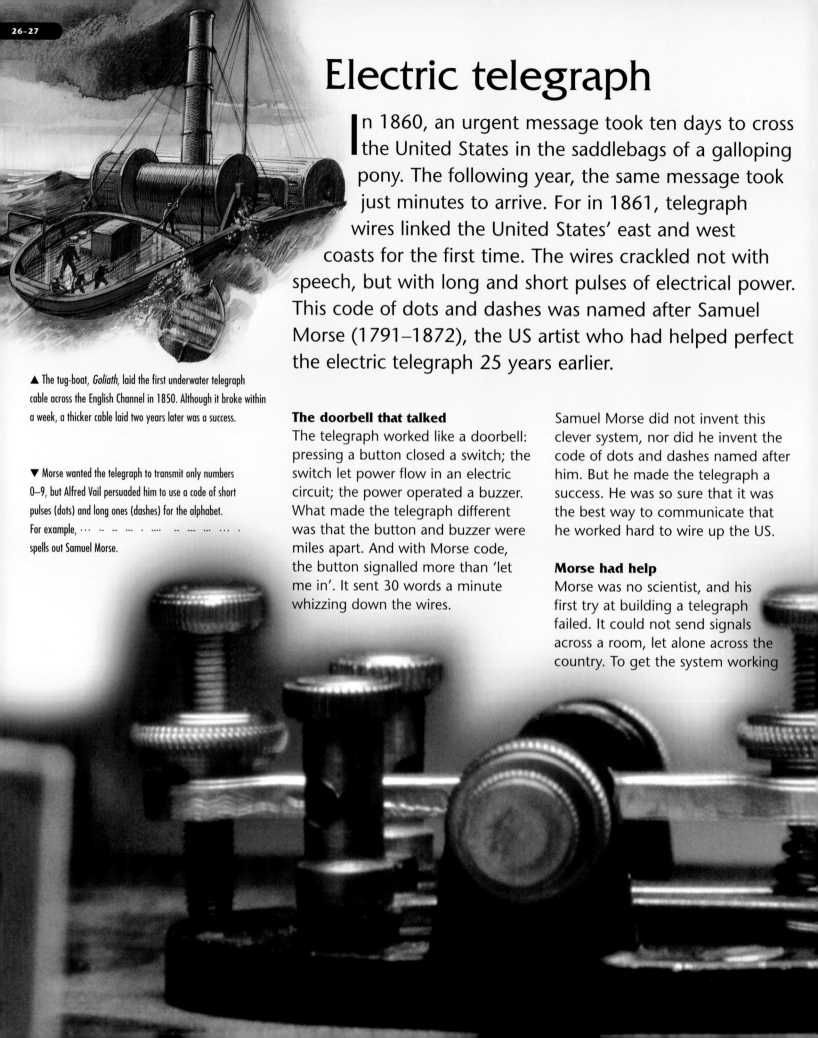

▲ The tug-boat, *Goliath*, laid the first underwater telegraph cable across the English Channel in 1850. Although it broke within a week, a thicker cable laid two years later was a success.

▼ Morse wanted the telegraph to transmit only numbers 0–9, but Alfred Vail persuaded him to use a code of short pulses (dots) and long ones (dashes) for the alphabet. For example, ··· ·· —— ··· · ···· —— ——— ·· ··· ·
spells out Samuel Morse.

The doorbell that talked

The telegraph worked like a doorbell: pressing a button closed a switch; the switch let power flow in an electric circuit; the power operated a buzzer. What made the telegraph different was that the button and buzzer were miles apart. And with Morse code, the button signalled more than 'let me in'. It sent 30 words a minute whizzing down the wires.

Samuel Morse did not invent this clever system, nor did he invent the code of dots and dashes named after him. But he made the telegraph a success. He was so sure that it was the best way to communicate that he worked hard to wire up the US.

Morse had help

Morse was no scientist, and his first try at building a telegraph failed. It could not send signals across a room, let alone across the country. To get the system working

◄ The telegraph gave American leaders instant news of victories and defeats in the country's Civil War (1861–5). Mobile telegraph units such as this one, laid enough cable to stretch half way around the world.

▼ Telegraph operators tapped a key to send messages. At the receiving station a machine printed the message out, but operators soon learned to 'read' the signal by listening to the clicks of the printer.

he called on chemistry professor Leonard Gail and student Alfred Vail. Together, they tested it by winding 16km of wire around a room.

Morse, Gail and Vail showed their telegraph to officials in Washington. The officials were impressed, and the partners won a grant of $30,000 to build a telegraph line linking the city to Baltimore 65km away. The next year saw lines link New York to four other cities. A frenzy of telegraph line building followed, and the network doubled in size every seven months.

Going global

This enthusiasm spread to other countries, as enterprising companies rushed to raise telegraph poles.

Copper wires strung between poles carried the signals from coast to coast... but no farther because it was impossible to build poles in the sea.

This problem was solved in 1850 with the development of a waterproof cable. The first one linked Britain with neighbouring France and, 16 years later, the world's biggest steamship, *Great Eastern*, unreeled a cable to link Europe and the US. By 1880, lines stretched around the world. Morse's dream of world-wide 'instantaneous communication' had come true.

Telephone

United States president Rutherford Hayes (1822–93) could not see the point of the telephone when he first made a call in 1876. In fact, he said, 'An amazing invention… but who would ever want to use one?' Fortunately, other people were more enthusiastic than President Hayes: by the end of the following year, the number of telephone users had grown from just six to 3,000. Four years later there were 133,000. Today, there are about 1,200 million telephones in use – and even more mobile telephones.

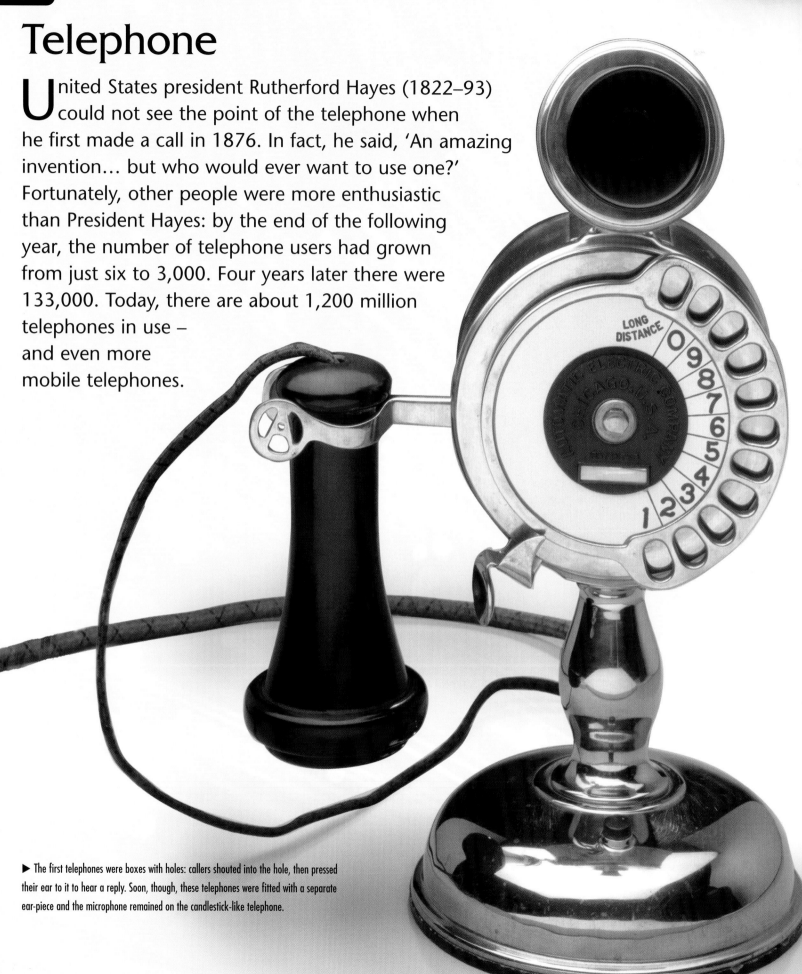

▶ The first telephones were boxes with holes: callers shouted into the hole, then pressed their ear to it to hear a reply. Soon, though, these telephones were fitted with a separate ear-piece and the microphone remained on the candlestick-like telephone.

◄ Telephones arrived just as women were winning equal rights with men, and the operator's job was among the first that was open to both sexes.

Inventive individuals
One United States immigrant built the first working telephone and another made the telephone system a success. In 1849, Italian-American Antonio Meucci (1808–96) was using electricity to treat a headache, when he discovered a way to send speech down the wires. He died before he could develop the telephone and it was left to the Scots-American Alexander Graham Bell (1847–1922) to perfect the device in 1876.

Telephones may have been new, but the network was not. Calls travelled down telegraph lines which had grown like a spider's web across the world over the previous 20 years.

Ask the operator
The first telephones connected to these lines had no dials. Callers had to ask an operator for the number.

This changed in 1891 when Almon Strowger (1839–1902) invented the automatic telephone exchange. He devised the exchange because his funeral business was not making money. He guessed that when people called the operator and asked for 'an undertaker', she was connecting the call to a rival. His automatic exchange solved the problem, allowing people to just dial the number they wanted. Because most telephone operators were women, he called his invention the 'girl-less, curse-less, out-of-order-less, wait-less telephone'.

Clicking switches
The undertaker's invention worked so well that it was used almost unchanged for 70 years. The world of telephones had moved on a long way by the time electronic exchanges replaced Almon Strowger's clicking switches.

In 1978, trials began of a radical new invention: the mobile telephone. At first, mobile telephones were costly and hard to come by because each one used a separate radio channel. However, new mobile telephones use computer technology to allow many mobiles to share fewer radio channels without interference.

Luxury telephones
Often we take for granted our ability to talk to friends at the touch of a button. But what is essential to us is impossible for many: half the people in the world cannot afford a telephone, and have never made a call.

▼ Radio beacons for mobile calls communicate with just a few telephones in a 'cell' – an area around the beacon.

▶ Today's mobiles have changed the way we communicate in ways that nobody could have guessed. Texting, for example, is a surprise success, creating a shorter, quicker way of writing brief messages.

SUMMARY OF CHAPTER 2: FROM ME TO YOU

A to Z of communication

The invention of the alphabet was a breakthrough in personal communication. Alphabets had one sign for each sound used in speech, so learning to write meant mastering fewer than 30 letters. The Phoenicians were probably the first to use an alphabet, in the 11th century BCE. The idea was copied by the Greeks, and later by the Romans who devised the alphabet we use today.

Alphabets did little to speed up long distance communications: messengers carried notes and letters on foot or on horseback. The great civilizations of Egypt, Rome and China all had official messenger services to deliver government communications. Private messenger services only began to thrive with the growth of business in 13th-century Europe. Public postal services appeared two centuries later in France and England. At first, only the rich could afford them, but they became more popular with the invention of the pre-paid letter delivered anywhere for the same low fee.

Speeding up the signal

For simple messages there were some quick alternatives to sending letters. Smoke or fire beacons helped people communicate almost instantly over short distances. By flashing sunlight off mirrors, or flying flags, it became possible to send quite long signals. A French inventor devised a chain of telegraph towers with flapping arms to keep the whole country in touch.

The electric telegraph replaced the semaphore system in the mid-19th century. The most successful telegraph was named after the US painter Samuel Morse. It was Morse who pioneered the network of wires and the dot-dash electrical pulses that flowed through them.

Speech began to travel down the same wires with the invention of the telephone in about 1870. All calls were connected by operators until an automatic exchange-and-dial telephone was invented. This system remained in use for 70 years. As it was becoming obsolete in the 1970s, a new kind of telephone was under development. Using radio waves rather than wires, it became the mobile telephone network that today rivals land-lines.

Go further...

View a family tree of alphabets:
www.ancientscripts.com/alphabet.html

Learn how communications technologies have grown from the telegraph to broadband:
www.connected-earth.com

Use the semaphore system:
www.anbg.gov.au/flags/semaphore

Samuel Morse and the Telegraph
by David Seidman
(Capstone press, 2008)

The Story of Thomas Alva Edison
by Margaret Cousins
(Random House, 1998)

Despatch rider
Delivers urgent documents and packages by bicycle or motorbike.

Network communications engineer
Uses knowledge of computer science and electrical and electronic engineering to design communications networks for voice and data.

Postal electronic technician
Installs and maintains sorting and processing equipment in mail centres.

Technical helpdesk advisor
Deals with customer and staff problems at a telephone company.

Explore the history of Britain's mail service:
Bath Postal Museum,
8 Broad Street,
Bath BA1 5JL.
Telephone: +44 (0) 1225 460333
www.bathpostalmuseum.org

See how Denmark's post and telephone services grew:
Danish Post and Telephone Museum,
Købmagergade 37 - Postbox 2053 -
DK 1012 Copenhagen.
Telephone: +45 33 41 09 00

Visit the inventor of the telephone, Antonio Meucci's home:
Garibaldi-Meucci Museum,
420 Tompkins Avenue,
Staten Island, NY 10305, USA.
www.garibaldimeuccimuseum.org

CHAPTER 3

Spreading the word

Sheets of white paper, tiny metal letters and sticky ink hardly seem like materials that could change the world. Yet, when Johannes Gutenberg (c.1400–68) first brought them together, that is exactly what happened. Communication was no longer personal, and ideas and knowledge spread rapidly. Although printing remained the most powerful way of communicating for about 400 years, in the 19th and 20th centuries, rivals appeared. Photography made lifelike copies of what we see, and then printed them. Film brought these still pictures to life. Recorded sound did for our ears what photography had done for our eyes, and radio transmitters sent speech and music around the world. Television has had an effect almost as dramatic as printing. In many countries, this bright and noisy box is the main source of news and entertainment.

Printing

Imagine copying a whole book by writing every word with a pen. It seems like an impossible task, yet all books were once made in this way. The introduction of printing in around 1440 put scribes out of work. In the time it took a scribe to write one costly book, a printer could make a thousand cheap ones. The new, printed books gave poorer people something to read and they spread radical new ideas that shook up the world of religion and science.

▲ Long before Gutenberg, pictures had been printed using blocks of wood carved with an image in reverse. Inking them and pressing on paper transferred the picture. However, carving words on a wood block was even slower than writing them by hand.

Printing pioneer

The German goldsmith, Johannes Gutenberg was responsible for this change in written communication. In about 1440, he started to make movable type – tiny lead blocks, each with one raised letter on top. Arranged to form sentences, and rolled with ink, the type transferred the text onto paper pressed against it.

▲ Movable type had only one letter on it. After one page had been printed, the letters could be taken apart, and rearranged to print the next page.

◀ Although Gutenberg's books were cheaper than hand-written ones, they still cost a clerk three years' wages. However, they did not make Gutenberg rich: in 1455, he failed to pay off a loan and went out of business.

▲ Alois Senefelder used a smooth block of limestone to print. Today's presses use printing plates instead. Curved around a drum, the plate turns constantly, pressing words and pictures onto the paper that passes under it.

Gutenberg did not actually invent printing – or the type, ink or paper. Simple printing from engraved seals began in China 2,700 years earlier, and the Chinese printer, Pi Cheng, made movable type from pottery four centuries before Gutenberg. However, Gutenberg *did* have one brilliant idea: he took a press used for smoothing out bed-sheets, and squeezed the paper and inky type together.

A revolution in knowledge
Gutenberg's idea had far-reaching effects. The following century, printed books spread the ideas of religious thinker Martin Luther (1483–1546). His challenge to the power of the pope split Christians into Protestants and Catholics. Printing also overturned long-held scientific beliefs, such as the idea that the universe turns around the earth. When Italian scientist Galileo Galilei (1564–1642) proved instead that the earth orbits the sun, he spread the news in a printed book.

Printing with wax and water
Movable type was the main way to print until the end of the 18th century. In 1796, Alois Senefelder (1771–1834)

used a wax crayon to write a laundry list on a slab of polished stone. He found that if he dampened the stone, ink from a roller stuck only to the waxy writing. Pressing paper onto the inky stone copied the text.

Giant presses
Today, most printing uses Senefelder's method, called 'lithography.' Instead of printing on single sheets of paper, the biggest presses now print on huge paper rolls. They print in colour by using a regular pattern of tiny dots coloured yellow, cyan (blue), magenta (pink) and black. Too small to see without a magnifying glass, the dots merge together to give the impression of a full-colour picture.

Digital or paper?
Ink on paper may seem old-fashioned in an age where the internet provides lightning-fast access to seemingly unlimited information. However, books, newspapers and magazines will be with us for a long time yet. After all, they need no battery power and you can read them anywhere. You can write on the pages – and unlike computers, they never crash!

▼ Today's printing presses are giants. Four storeys high, they print on a strip of paper as wide as a bed-sheet. In one hour, this machine can print, trim and fold 80,000 copies of a 96-page newspaper in full colour.

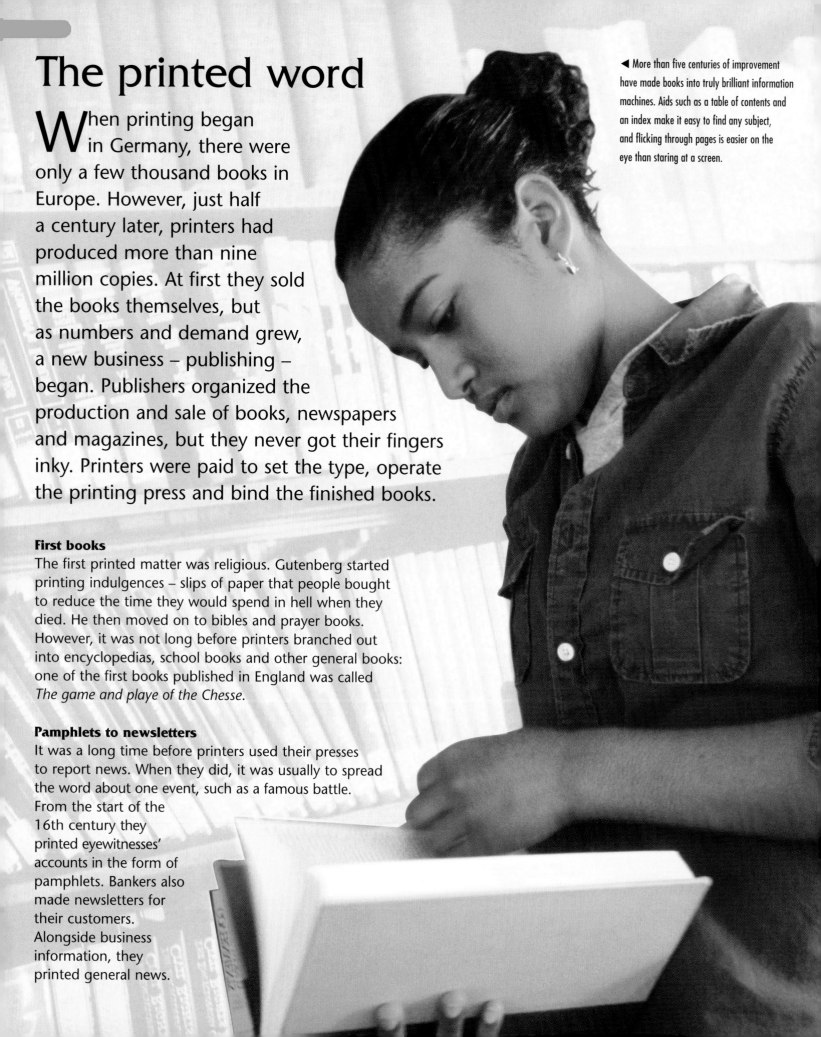

The printed word

When printing began in Germany, there were only a few thousand books in Europe. However, just half a century later, printers had produced more than nine million copies. At first they sold the books themselves, but as numbers and demand grew, a new business – publishing – began. Publishers organized the production and sale of books, newspapers and magazines, but they never got their fingers inky. Printers were paid to set the type, operate the printing press and bind the finished books.

First books

The first printed matter was religious. Gutenberg started printing indulgences – slips of paper that people bought to reduce the time they would spend in hell when they died. He then moved on to bibles and prayer books. However, it was not long before printers branched out into encyclopedias, school books and other general books: one of the first books published in England was called *The game and playe of the Chesse*.

Pamphlets to newsletters

It was a long time before printers used their presses to report news. When they did, it was usually to spread the word about one event, such as a famous battle. From the start of the 16th century they printed eyewitnesses' accounts in the form of pamphlets. Bankers also made newsletters for their customers. Alongside business information, they printed general news.

◄ More than five centuries of improvement have made books into truly brilliant information machines. Aids such as a table of contents and an index make it easy to find any subject, and flicking through pages is easier on the eye than staring at a screen.

Newspapers spread

The bankers' publications came out only occasionally. Real newspapers that appeared regularly began circulating about a century later. The first was probably the monthly *Relation of Select and Noteworthy Happenings*, published in Strasbourg, Germany, in 1609. Other publishers in Germany and the Netherlands quickly copied the idea. However, the newspaper was slower to spread beyond Europe. Even in 1866 an international traveller from Japan to Europe had to explain to his friends at home what a newspaper was. He told them that from it, a reader could learn about current events '… though he remains indoors, and does not see what goes on outside.'

Today, newspapers and books are published just about everywhere. World-wide, 84,000 newspapers are published daily, and about 550 million people read them. There is just as much variety in books and magazines: 850,000 new book titles are published each year.

▼ Putting a daily newspaper together is a nailbiting job. Editors and designers have only a few hours to organize pictures and stories from around the corner and from around the world. The newspaper has to be printed overnight so that it is ready for sale on news-stands, by dawn.

Comics and cartoons

The first thing many people do when they open the newspaper, is turn to the funnies. Amusing drawings are nearly 500 years old, but comic strips only began in 1896 with the publication of *The Yellow Kid* in a New York newspaper. The story of this poor child was aimed at adults, and it boosted the paper's sales. This is still true today: the best comics amuse everyone, and – as 'graphic novels' – comics are bought and read by both children and serious collectors.

Publishing people

Putting together a newspaper or magazine takes a staggering amount of work. Journalists, photographers and illustrators provide the raw material, and experts at publishing houses prepare it for printing. Editors choose what will be included and graphic designers decide what the pages will look like. They work with picture researchers who find photographs and illustrations in picture libraries. Finally, production staff gather everything together and send it to the printers.

◄ When recording a live performance, sound engineers usually aim for the most accurate copy of what the audience hears. By routing the signals from each microphone and instrument pick-up to a separate recording track, they can adjust and balance the overall sound later.

Recording sound

Soaring guitar riffs and a pounding bass throb from today's tiny MP3 players. Although this digital technology is changing how we buy and use recorded sound, it has not eliminated vinyl. The shiny black plastic discs that still dominate the dance floor have a surprisingly long history. They first appeared in 1888, and spun almost unaltered for more than a century. Recorded sound itself is even older. It began in the laboratory of Thomas Edison (1847–1931).

The machine that spoke

Edison had the idea of recording sound in the summer of 1877. The 'talking machine' he sketched had a cylinder covered in tin foil with a crank to turn it. His engineer built the machine, and to everyone's surprise, it worked first time. By turning the cylinder while shouting into a funnel, Edison indented the tin foil with a wiggly groove. Each wiggle copied the pulses of air pressure that make up sounds. To play back the sound, he used another needle that followed the grooves, amplifying its movements with a stretched paper disc. Edison never dreamed his simple invention would amount to much,

describing it as 'a mere toy'. He was almost right. Although, at first, his phonograph astonished the public, the novelty wore off quickly.

The first discs

What turned sound recording from a toy into a way of playing and selling music was an invention that came some ten years later. German-American Émile Berliner (1851–1925) replaced Edison's cylinders with flat discs. They were more compact and did not wear out as quickly as the cylinders. But most importantly, they were easy to make. From a metal 'master' disc, Berliner could press thousands of identical copies.

Magnetic sound

Like Edison's system, Berliner's players were mechanical: they did not use electricity. Electrical recording began when Danish engineer Valdemar Poulsen (1869–1942) invented the 'telegraphone' in 1898. This stored sound in a reel of iron wire, magnetized in a pattern that copied the pulses of speech and music.

Digital music

Poulsen's invention was used mainly as a telephone answering machine, and hardly affected recorded music at first. Berliner's discs continued to be the main way of playing music at home until the introduction of the compact disc (CD), by the Sony and Phillips corporations, in 1983. These discs stored music digitally – as computer data – eliminating the clicks and pops of vinyl.

CDs are still a favourite way of playing music, but this is changing fast. A quiet revolution in music started in 1989 when Germany's Fraunhofer Institute found a way to make music data files ten times smaller. As MP3s, songs are easy to swap on the internet and download onto pocket-size electronic jukeboxes. Soon MP3s may make CDs look as old fashioned as Edison's cylinders.

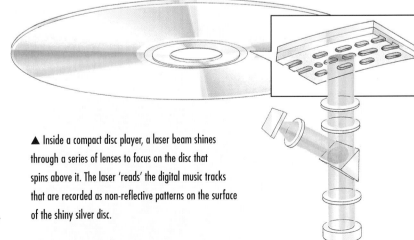

▲ Inside a compact disc player, a laser beam shines through a series of lenses to focus on the disc that spins above it. The laser 'reads' the digital music tracks that are recorded as non-reflective patterns on the surface of the shiny silver disc.

▲ Daguerre used a camera like this one, as did William Fox Talbot (1800–77), an Englishman who invented a different photographic process independently of Daguerre.

▲ A modern digital camera is a tiny computer with a lens. A light-sensitive silicon chip inside the camera captures images, shows them on the tiny screen, and saves them to a memory card.

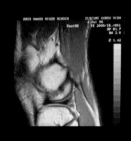

▲ Medical instruments that look inside the body make pictures similar to photographs. These images, created using computerised axial tomography (CAT) scanning, help doctors to detect brain tumours.

Photography

It is hard to imagine a world without photography. Perhaps we could give up snapshots, but magazines would look dull if drawings and paintings were their only pictures. Photography is used not only for entertainment, but also for communication. Special cameras etch the patterns on silicon chips used in computers and television – equipment vital for communication. In hospitals, doctors would have to live without X-rays and CAT scans because both of these use kinds of photography.

The first photographer

In the first week of January 1839, French scene painter Louis Daguerre (1789–1851) suddenly became one of the most famous men in Paris. Daguerre had invented a mirror with a memory. He had found a way to make shiny silver plates record perfect, lifelike pictures inside a camera. Fellow French artists were astonished and alarmed, and one artist commented 'from today, painting is dead!' For until Daguerre's invention, the only way to create a picture was with a brush or a pencil – and a great deal of skill.

Colour and movement

In fact, artists had nothing to fear. Daguerre could only photograph objects that stood perfectly still; even

◄ Although modern cameras are easy to use, taking photographs for magazines, newspapers and advertisements still requires skill and extensive training. Here the photographer is using elaborate lighting to shoot a fashion picture, with help from an assistant and a hair-stylist.

the leaves on trees were blurred and portraits were impossible. The 'Daguerrotypes', as the shiny pictures were called, were in black and white. However, improvements to photography gradually removed these handicaps and by 1877, it was possible to take a photograph of a galloping horse. Colour photography took another 30 years to perfect.

Snapshots!

For a long time, taking pictures meant buying a lot of expensive equipment. Photographers developed and printed their own pictures in darkrooms – special rooms that do not let in light. Then, in 1888, the US inventor George Eastman (1854–1932) began to sell box-shaped cameras

made of cardboard. With the slogan 'you press the button, we do the rest', Eastman made photography trouble free. His cardboard 'Kodaks' were just like today's disposable cameras. When the film was finished, you posted the whole camera back to the maker, who printed the pictures.

Photography now

This clever idea meant that you did not have to be an expert photographer to take good pictures. Eastman started the snapshot industry that today allows us to capture and share pictures of happy moments. Although photography began with a camera, lens, light and film, to take good photographs today, you do not need all these things.

Digital cameras and many scientific image-making instruments use electronic sensors instead of film. And by replacing light with magnetic fields, infra-red beams or X-rays, we can see deep inside the human body – and look at the farthest corners of the universe.

These special uses of photography expand our knowledge and save lives. However, the main value of the camera is still in communication and entertainment. Despite the advance of television and cinema, images in newspapers and magazines still have greater power to anger, shock and amuse us. By capturing a moment in time, photography gives us a unique view of the world that moving pictures can never quite match.

In *Harry Potter and The Chamber of Secrets*, computer graphics give Harry Potter extra help when he misses the Hogwarts express. But when the flying car swoops realistically through the arches of the viaduct, it is hard not to believe in magic.

Cinema

When cars fly through the air, or an action hero seems about to die, we know that what we are watching on the movie screen is not real. But the magic of cinema is so powerful that we all gasp and sit on the edge of our seats, our hearts pounding with excitement. This ability to thrill, surprise and terrify audiences has helped to keep cinemas full ever since motion pictures first hit the big screen in 1895.

▼ Pushing a coin into one of Thomas Edison's kinetoscopes showed a 20-second-long film that only one person at a time could watch. The US inventor thought that projected films were no threat to his one-at-a-time peepshows. Foolishly, he refused to project his films, saying, 'If we make this screen machine, it will spoil everything.'

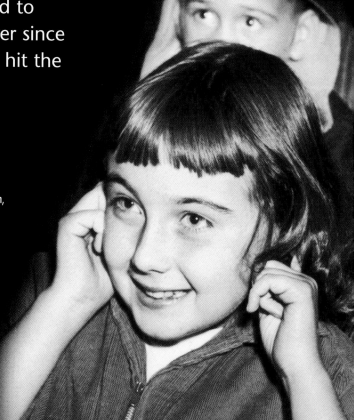

▶ Cinema is one of the most powerful ways of communicating. The darkness, the huge screen, and the loud, surrounding sound block out all other thoughts and senses. No wonder we cover our eyes at the scary scenes!

Moving picture toys

Motion pictures did not begin with the first cinema. More than 150 years earlier, scientists had shown that if we flick quickly enough through a series of slightly different drawings, we do not see any one picture clearly. Instead, the pictures seem to move as if alive.

Not quite a movie

The invention of photography (see page 38) made this trick even more real. In 1878, England's Eadweard Muybridge (1830–1904) used 12 cameras to take a dozen photographs of a speeding horse in just half a second. Flashed quickly in front of viewers, the horse galloped realistically. Although Muybridge's invention was limited to a couple of seconds of movement, he inspired inventors and they looked for ways to show longer sequences.

Film on a loop

The first inventor to have any real success was William Dickson (1860–1935), who worked in the laboratory of Thomas Edison. Dickson built a camera that could take an endless series of photographs on a roll of film, and show them in rapid sequence to recreate movement. Edison told Dickson what to do, then patented the system himself as the 'kinetoscope'.

Screen machine

Although the kinetoscope showed real movies, it was the work of two French brothers that turned cinema into an art form. Auguste (1862–1954) and Louis Lumière (1864–1948) had the brilliant idea of projecting movies onto a screen in a darkened room, so that many people could watch the film together. At one of their first film viewings in 1895, they showed an express train rushing towards the camera. Some members of the audience were so terrified that they ran for the exit!

Sound and colour

The Lumière brothers' films, and the thousands that followed them, were not only in black and white, but they were also silent. Printed text appeared on screen to explain what people were saying, and a pianist or orchestra provided musical accompaniment. The first films with sound appeared in 1900, and true-colour movies were only made 17 years later.

Although the invention of television and video cut film audiences, people still queue to see the latest blockbusters on the big screen. It is easy to see why cinemas remain full: television just cannot compete with the experience of watching movies on a giant screen, and sharing the thrills, excitement and tears with hundreds of other film fans.

Using studios, outside-broadcast units and recordings, radio stations mix news, music, sport, discussion, drama and entertainment. Taxes pay for public-service stations such as the BBC and advertising (see page 58) covers the cost of broadcasts from other stations.

Radio

Think of radio and you probably think of a portable radio belting out music on the beach. But radio does much more than entertain us. Tiny radio chips cordlessly connect our portable telephone calls and computer printers. Radio waves are used to send distress signals from sinking ships, to communicate with spacecraft, and to navigate on land, at sea and in the air. In fact, without radio, we would literally be lost!

Radio was first used by crews onboard ships to communicate with each other. But when the *Titanic* sank in 1912, other ships overlooked the distress signals broadcast by her radio operator (played here by an actor), and about 1,500 people drowned. After the *Titanic* disaster, laws were passed that forced all ships to keep their radios on day and night.

Guglielmo Marconi

The man who made modern-day radio possible was the Italian student, Guglielmo Marconi (1874–1937). Marconi realized that radio waves could be used to replace telegraph wires (see page 26) and began experimenting at home in 1894. Using very simple equipment, he managed to send a radio signal across a room, then to the end of the garden. Next, his brother carried a home-made radio receiver out of sight to the neighbouring valley. When he received Guglielmo's signals, he replied by firing a hunting gun in the air.

Long distance signals

Marconi's invention was called 'wireless telegraphy', because it sent Morse code messages without the wires that connected telegraph stations. Wireless telegraphy seemed a natural way to communicate with ships, but unfortunately, Guglielmo could not interest anyone in Italy in his work. So he travelled to England to develop his idea. There, he signalled over longer and longer distances: across London, across a flat plain and across the sea. Triumphantly, in 1901, he sent a signal across the Atlantic Ocean.

▶ Radio waves have different frequencies (channels) and each one carries a different radio station. So by tuning in a radio set, we can listen to many different stations. And, unlike most entertainment, we pay nothing.

Words and music

Marconi's 'wireless' sent only Morse code. But radio became more interesting in 1906 when United States inventor Reginald Fessenden (1866–1932) transmitted speech and music. His signals surprised radio operators on nearby ships, who had never heard anything but the crackle of dots and dashes in their headphones.

Fessenden's breakthrough made the radio broadcasts that we take for granted possible. Early radio signals usually connected two individual stations, allowing them to exchange messages. But radio broadcasts were different. A single radio station sent out the signals, while hundreds, thousands or even millions of people with radio receivers listened in. Regular broadcasts began in the US around 1920, and KDKA in Pittsburgh was one of the first stations on the air.

Digital future

Today, radio waves help us in so many ways that we hardly realize we are using them. Following the invention of integrated circuits (silicon chips) in around 1960, radio sets became smaller and cheaper. Computers and digital technology enabled engineers to make even better use of radio. And in a twist that might make Marconi laugh, today's digital radio is broadcast as a series of on-off pulses – much like his original Morse code signals.

▶ Unlike waves in water, or sound waves in air, radio waves do not need a material to travel through. This enables broadcasts from earth to reach out into space, keeping us in touch with astronauts such as Dr Mamoru Mohri during Mission STS-47 in 1992.

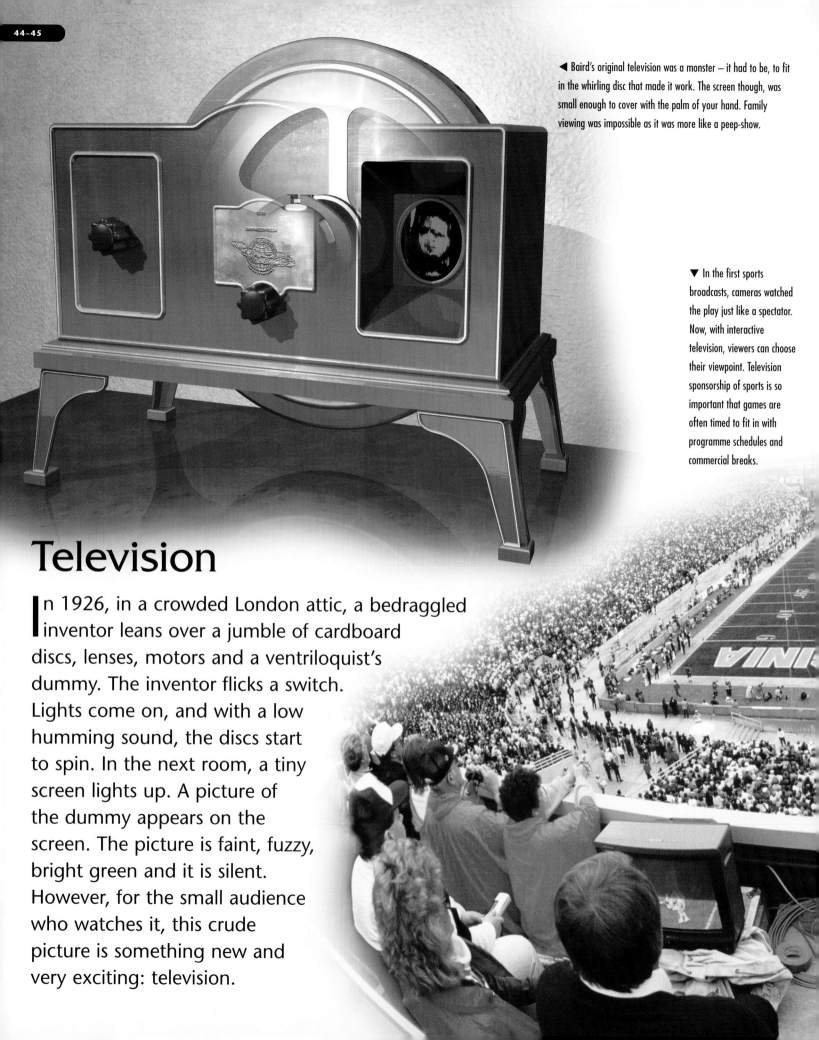

◀ Baird's original television was a monster – it had to be, to fit in the whirling disc that made it work. The screen though, was small enough to cover with the palm of your hand. Family viewing was impossible as it was more like a peep-show.

▼ In the first sports broadcasts, cameras watched the play just like a spectator. Now, with interactive television, viewers can choose their viewpoint. Television sponsorship of sports is so important that games are often timed to fit in with programme schedules and commercial breaks.

Television

In 1926, in a crowded London attic, a bedraggled inventor leans over a jumble of cardboard discs, lenses, motors and a ventriloquist's dummy. The inventor flicks a switch. Lights come on, and with a low humming sound, the discs start to spin. In the next room, a tiny screen lights up. A picture of the dummy appears on the screen. The picture is faint, fuzzy, bright green and it is silent. However, for the small audience who watches it, this crude picture is something new and very exciting: television.

Wireless picture pioneer

The inventor was John Logie Baird (1888–1946), a Scotsman whose demonstration impressed those who saw it. Baird himself was sure that what he called the 'televisor' would really work. But not everyone believed him. When Baird took his invention to a newspaper office, the editor ordered his assistant to 'go down to reception and get rid of a lunatic who's down there. He says he's got a machine for seeing by wireless!'

Promising start – no future

But Baird pressed on, and with a winning mix of confidence, inventiveness and cheek, he was granted a licence for television broadcasts. The BBC started trial programmes in 1929, but only 30 people watched them – two thirds of them using television sets they had made themselves!

Baird's whirling disc sets attracted a lot of attention in Britain, but he could not compete with an all-electronic system invented in the US. When regular broadcasts began – in Britain and abroad – viewers watched them not on Baird's quaint televisor, but on electronic sets with no moving parts from the giant CBS, RCA and EMI corporations.

▲ As anyone who has 'channel surfed' cable or satellite television knows, more channels does not always mean better viewing, because good television programmes are expensive to produce. Though this technician at the television station monitors up to 90 channels, many show programmes of little interest to most viewers.

The colourful fifties

These first television programmes were in black and white. Although research on colour television had begun in the 1930s, it was a long time before the pictures were as clear as on black-and-white sets. Colour television broadcasts began in the United States in 1951, but, just as with Baird's programmes 20 years earlier, only about two dozen people had sets that could receive them. It was not until 1971 that sales of colour television sets overtook those of black-and-white sets.

Television today

The television sets we watch our favourite programmes on today are much bigger and brighter than those of the 1970s. However, the biggest change has been in what we watch, not how we watch it. Satellite and cable television allow us to see a huge variety of programmes about all kinds of special interests and hobbies. Equally as important, cable technology also allows television companies to broadcast programmes to just one town – and to provide its citizens with their own channel and regional news.

Now, with digital video cameras (see page 46), and a little training and practice, anyone can make and show a television programme. Sit and watch the box for long enough, and sooner or later you will see your friends, your town – maybe even yourself – on screen!

Video and DVD

Television has become such an important part of our lives that the familiar faces on the screen feel like friends. Better still, with a video cassette recorder (VCR) or digital versatile disc (DVD) player, we can meet up with them at any time. However, it was not always like this: before video, people had to rush home to watch their favourite shows. Video has affected television in another important way: with a video camera, we can leap beyond the television set and create our own programmes. With digital video we can use a home computer to make them almost as polished as a Hollywood movie.

And now, on tape...

Today, live television shows are rare, but until the 1950s, all television shows were broadcast exactly as they happened. This caused problems for broadcasters in the United States. There, because of the different time zones, viewers in New York would have to stay awake until midnight to watch a sports match played at 9pm in Los Angeles. In 1956, engineers at the US Ampex Corporation changed this when they found a way to record television pictures and sound onto magnetic tape. The tape was as wide as a credit card and snaked between two huge, open spools. These recorders were so vast and expensive that only the biggest television companies could afford them.

Convenient cassettes

Home video recording began 20 years later with the launch of the 'video home system' (VHS) by the giant Japanese electronics company, Matsushita. They produced plastic video cassettes that enclosed spools of narrower tape. Pushing a cassette into the VCR and pressing the record button, triggered the machine to pull out the tape and lace it round the drum that recorded and played back the television signal.

▶ Home video has changed how we remember the past. Memories may fade, but in the red, green and blue lines of a television picture, a video shows us for what we are — heroes or horrors — five, ten or 20 years later.

Time shifting

The first VCRs were expensive, but the price soon fell and they became popular as a way of watching pre-recorded movies. Viewers also used VCRs for time-shifting – recording programmes to watch them at a more convenient moment. Today, DVDs are replacing video cassettes for watching the latest blockbusters. Though they look similar to compact discs (CDs), DVDs hold much more information: in addition to a film, they may also contain trailers, games, or even a soundtrack in another language.

Lights... camera... ACTION!

If VCRs changed the way we watch television, then home video cameras did something more important. They changed how we see and remember ourselves and our families. Home movies were hardly new when home video cameras appeared, but shooting a home movie was slow and costly. Cameras held only four minutes of film, which needed processing before you could set up a projector, darken the room and watch it. Video, by contrast, provided instant replay on an ordinary television.

The dawn of digital

Early video cameras were big and heavy, and linked to a separate recorder by a thick cable. One piece 'camcorders' appeared in 1982. The newest camcorders store images and sound digitally. They are tiny and accessible, but more importantly, they make video editing simple. By copying a video onto a computer, you can cut out blunders and dull shots, and add music, sound effects and titles. Carefully 'cutting' a video can turn it from a two-hour yawn into an action-packed, 20-minute, real-life drama!

▶ Using computer software such as Apple's iMovie, you can change the order of video shots, fade between them, and add new scenes shot later in different places. When your editing is done, you can burn the finished movie onto a DVD.

SUMMARY OF CHAPTER 3: SPREADING THE WORD

A new way to put words on paper

Until the invention of the printing press, writing was the only way to copy and spread information. The press led to an explosion of knowledge, and printers developed the book into a form that was useful for both reference and entertainment. Although printing methods have improved, books themselves have scarcely changed.

At first, the printers sold the books they made, but with time, publishers began to organize book production. They paid the author and printer, and then sold the books to shops. Publishers also made pamphlets, newspapers and magazines. Together, these printed communications reached millions of people.

New ways of multiplying information did not appear until the 19th century. The camera spread pictures as efficiently as the printing press spread words. Developed about 160 years ago, at first photography captured only rock-steady subjects in shades of grey. Action photography had to wait 30 years, and colour photography, 60 years.

Inventing a talking machine

Sound recording was the idea of Thomas Edison, but his 1877 cylinder recorder was a toy. Discs invented 10 years later made sound recording popular – today's digital CDs replaced them only in the 1980s. It was also Edison who pioneered moving pictures with a coin-operated viewer. Projected movies first threw the images on the big screen in 1895, with sound following soon after.

We owe the discovery of radio to Guglielmo Marconi. Marconi could not interest anyone in the wireless telegraph in his native Italy, so he took it to Britain. There, he sent signals over long distances, and in 1901, the signals spanned the Atlantic. Five years later, the transmission of speech and music made the news and entertainment broadcasts we enjoy today possible.

Transmitting pictures was a dream until the 1920s, when the televisor was invented. Its spinning disc made tiny pictures, but with the development of electronic television, it was quickly forgotten. With the addition of colour, and videotape recording, television has become the most powerful communications tool yet invented.

Go further...

See a copy of a Gutenberg Bible:
www.hrc.utexas.edu/
permanent/gutenberg/

View early photography:
www.mccord-museum.qc.ca/
en/keys/webtours/VQ_PI_I_EN

Read about the early days
of motion pictures:
www.americanhistory.si.edu/
cinema

Find out how the British Broadcasting Corporation (BBC) transmitted its very first radio programme:
www.sciencemuseum.org.uk/
exhibitions/2lo

Book editor
Plans and co-ordinates printed books in collaboration with authors, illustrators and designers, then checks and corrects the text.

Journalist
Collects news and other stories for broadcast media, such as television, newspapers and magazines.

Photographic assistant
Helps to run a photographic studio, assisting the photographer during all aspects of a shoot.

Sound recording engineer
Transfers an artist's performance to tape, and helps mix the sound to a finished recording, ready for release.

See communication exhibits: Science Museum, Exhibition Road, London SW7 2DD.
Telephone: +44 (0) 870 870 4868
www.sciencemuseum.org.uk

See a recreation of Gutenberg's printing press in his home town:
Gutenberg Museum,
5 Liebfrauenplats Mainz,
Rhineland-Palatinate,
Germany.
Telephone: +49 (0) 613 1232 955

Visit the house where Thomas Edison was born:
9 Edison Drive, Milan,
Ohio, USA.
Telephone: +1 419 499 2135
www.tomedison.org

CHAPTER 4

The global village

The phrase 'global village' was first used to describe a world wired for instant communication. In a global village, talking to someone on the other side of the earth would be easy – as if the globe had shrunk to the size of a village. In this chapter, you can trace the progress of the technologies, such as satellites and the internet, that made the global village a reality.

As communications have become more widespread, the urge to control them has also increased. The internet makes this difficult. Distributed around the world in a million computers, it is everywhere, and yet nowhere. If one computer is switched off, messages and web pages flow another way to their destination. This self-healing ability makes the web open and free-for-all. However, openness is not always an advantage. You can never be sure whether your messages are safe. This is an age-old problem and the speed of communications has made it more important than ever.

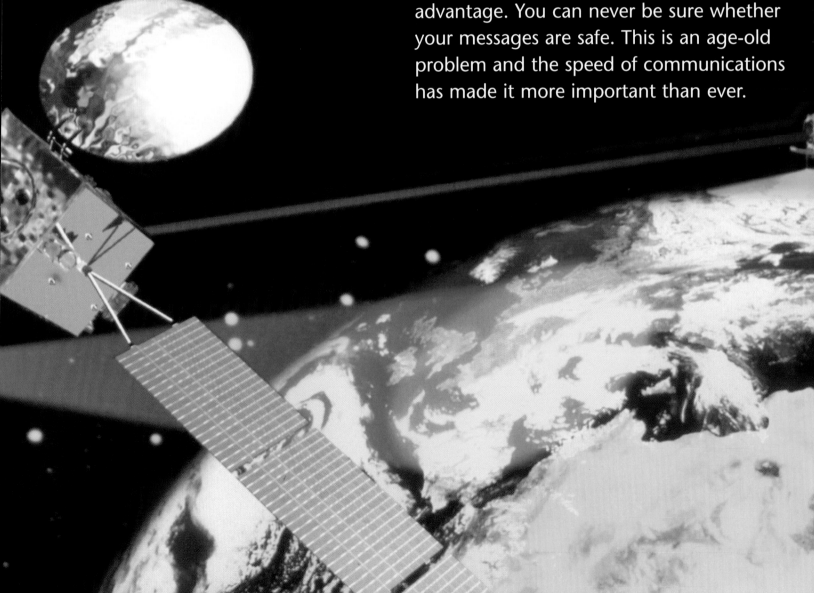

Satellites

Look at the sky at dusk or dawn, and you may see a bright speck move quickly across it. It is not a shooting star or a comet, but a satellite orbiting the earth. Satellites like these are vital links in communications networks: they relay telephone calls, broadcast television programmes and provide internet connections. The satellites you can see are in low earth orbit, about 80km up. However, most communications satellites circle much higher than this and they orbit at the same speed that the earth turns, so they seem to hover, as if stationary, above the Equator.

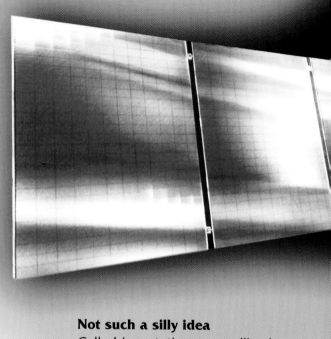

▼ Powered by unfolding solar panels, communications satellites are like orbiting radio stations, relaying microwave signals between ground stations on opposite sides of the globe. Earth's gravity keeps them trapped in orbit, stopping them from spinning off into space.

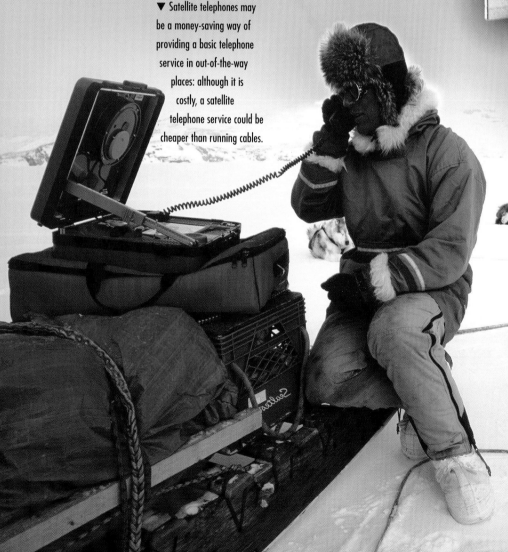

▼ Satellite telephones may be a money-saving way of providing a basic telephone service in out-of-the-way places: although it is costly, a satellite telephone service could be cheaper than running cables.

Not such a silly idea

Called 'geostationary satellites', these orbiting craft were the idea of science fiction writer Arthur C Clarke (b.1917). In 1945, he suggested launching satellites to exactly 35,900km, where they would orbit the earth just once a day. There they could receive radio signals broadcast from a base station on earth, and retransmit them to another distant spot on the ground.

At the time, people made fun of Clarke, because satellites had never been launched. But Clarke had the last laugh. For within 20 years, a satellite called *Early Bird* began relaying telephone calls and television pictures exactly as he had predicted.

A new way of talking

Satellites quickly changed the way we communicate. Within 15 years, they carried more than two thirds

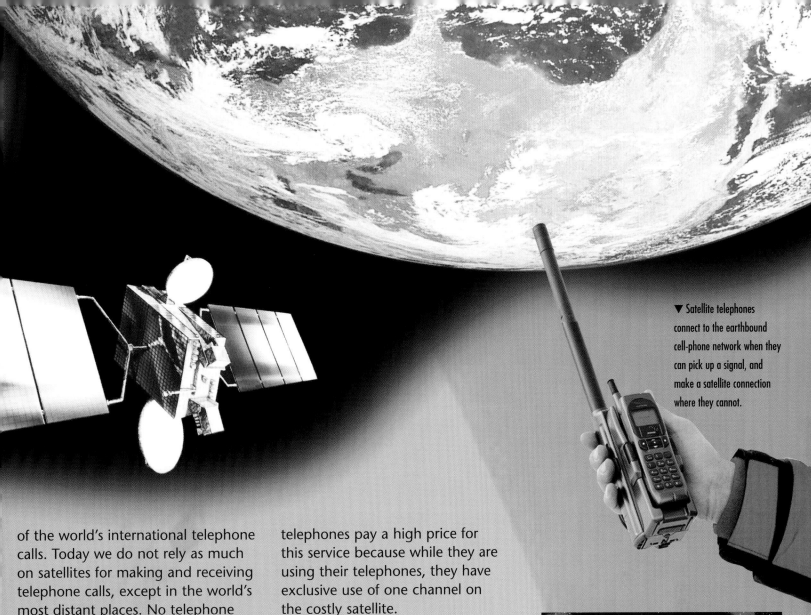

▼ Satellite telephones connect to the earthbound cell-phone network when they can pick up a signal, and make a satellite connection where they cannot.

of the world's international telephone calls. Today we do not rely as much on satellites for making and receiving telephone calls, except in the world's most distant places. No telephone cables reach these remote areas, and they are out of range of the beacons that provide mobile telephone coverage (see page 28). Satellites fill the gap, allowing explorers and soldiers to call home.

'Sorry to keep you waiting…'

The satellite telephones that use geostationary satellites need to be extremely powerful because the satellite is so far away. Calls made and received using the telephones also have awkward delays because the signal takes about half a second to reach the satellite and return to earth. However, a new generation of telephones has overcome these problems by using satellites much closer to earth. Users of satellite telephones pay a high price for this service because while they are using their telephones, they have exclusive use of one channel on the costly satellite.

Television in orbit

Compared to the cost of satellite telephone calls, satellite television is cheap and readily available. It uses geostationary satellites to beam television signals to small regions of the earth's surface. Because millions of television viewers receive the same satellite channels, they share the high cost of the satellite and broadcasting system, and each viewer pays very little for the service.

The first home satellite television systems, introduced in 1983, needed receiving dishes as big as beach umbrellas, but the most modern systems use rooftop dishes hardly bigger than a dinner plate.

▲ The Iridium phone system uses 66 satellites in low earth orbit. Each satellite circles the earth every 100 minutes. The system eliminates delays in speech, and it is the only way to make telephone calls from the poles and other distant places.

The internet

Spreading across the globe in a tangled and complicated mesh, the internet connects hundreds of millions of computers. The beauty of this giant communications network is that to use it, we do not need to know a lot about it. Just clicking a button can connect us to friends across the globe – or around the corner. The internet's creators never dreamed it would be used to book cinema tickets, order a take-away meal, or play games such as chess. This amazing technology began as a way to protect the United States from missile attack.

Missiles and radar

During the 1950s and 1960s, the United States and the USSR threatened each other with missiles of terrifying power – this battle became known as the Cold War. To protect their country, US scientists built radar stations to warn of an attack, and rockets to knock Russian missiles out of the sky. To connect the radar to the missile bases, they created a complicated computer network called SAGE. The network was extremely slow – today's modems transfer data 50 times faster – but it worked.

▲ Not only is the internet a useful source of information, but it is also a source of endless entertainment. Games, such as chess, can be played with friends who are at the same school or on the other side of the world.

▲ Inside huge domes like this one, radar dishes scanned the skies for approaching missiles. The first computer networks linked the radar dishes to missiles, allowing United States army chiefs to mount revenge attacks if US cities were threatened.

Making it bullet proof

When engineers improved the original system, they added a clever twist. The network that replaced SAGE was bullet-proof. If a missile struck part of the new network, the data automatically found a way around the damage.

In the late 1960s, US Department of Defense scientists adapted the system to share research information, creating ARPANET. Large universities, and then smaller institutions, joined the network. By 1983, what we now call the internet was almost complete.

The world-wide-web

Using ARPANET was not easy: you had to key in complex commands for it to work. This changed in the early 1990s when British scientist Tim Berners-Lee (b.1955) created the first web browser – finding information became as easy as pointing and clicking. Soon afterwards, Mark Andreesen (b.1971) adapted Berners-Lee's program to run on both Apple Macintoshes (Macs) and personal computers (PCs), calling it Mosaic.

Super-quick messages

A speedy rival to the postal system appeared in 1971 when engineer Ray Tomlinson (b.1941) invented email. Working on ARPANET, he worked out a way for researchers to leave messages on each other's computers. He chose the @ sign to separate a computer user's address from the name of their network because it 'seemed to make sense… the user was "at" some other network'.

Together, browsers and email made the internet simple and appealing, and the number of internet users grew rapidly. Each year, the internet doubles in size as people discover that it can be a library, a jukebox, a postman, a cinema, a supermarket… and a thousand other useful, entertaining things.

Merging media

How would you like to store your favourite tracks on your wristwatch? Or see live football on your mobile telephone? Or even read the newspaper on your refrigerator door? As communications become faster and smarter, devices such as telephones, televisions, personal computers and fax machines are becoming more and more alike. Many magazines and newspapers now have electronic editions. A single shiny disc can replace a whole shelf of heavy encyclopedias. The only limit on how we will use communications technologies in the future is our imagination.

Fancy phones

Clever software and shrinking computer chips have blurred the differences between the gadgets that we use to communicate. Not long ago, we had to use a camera to take holiday snap shots, a computer to surf the web, a mobile phone to call friends and a personal stereo to listen to music. Now, the smallest mobile telephones can do all these things.

Wired telephones are also merging with computers and the internet. Telecommunication companies are already routing some long distance calls over the internet. With a little ingenuity, it is possible to use a computer to chat to friends on the other side of the world – free of charge.

No hi-fi needed

Home entertainment is moving in the same direction. By linking a music system to a home network, you can play MP3s stored on a computer in another room. Listening to the radio on-line, you can hear local programmes from your own country or anywhere in the world.

Printed pages

Newspapers and magazines could merge with the electronic world in unusual ways. Although reading a magazine on the web is hardly a new experience, what about a newspaper with images that move? Or a whole magazine printed on a single sheet of paper? Digital paper may soon make these things possible. It feels just like regular paper, but its ink appears and disappears under computer control.

The pros and cons

How useful are these devices and new ways of communicating? There is little point in owning a telephone that does everything, if it cannot do anything well.

Figuring out what is useful, and what is not, will take some time, but new media are pointing the way. You can subscribe to electronic newspapers that show you only articles on subjects that interest you.

▼ MP3s combine music with the internet. By downloading individual songs off the web, you can buy the best and skip the rest.

New video recorders download television schedules, and record episodes of your favourite show that you have missed.

Simple but safe

Some of the most successful ideas are also the simplest. The short messaging service (SMS) or text messaging was, at first, a minor feature of mobile telephones. However, this joining of the scribbled note and the telephone, has created a tool that many of us rely on. So, as technologies move closer together, it may be the smallest things that change communications in the most amazing ways.

▲ Although it is time-consuming jotting notes on a personal organizer, a paper diary and address book would make a much bigger bulge in your pocket. Speech recognition may eventually create an organizer that takes dictation.

▼ Merging television, the internet and telephones, video-conferencing does more than bring scattered workers together. It also links remote schools in the Australian outback to teachers over 1,500km away.

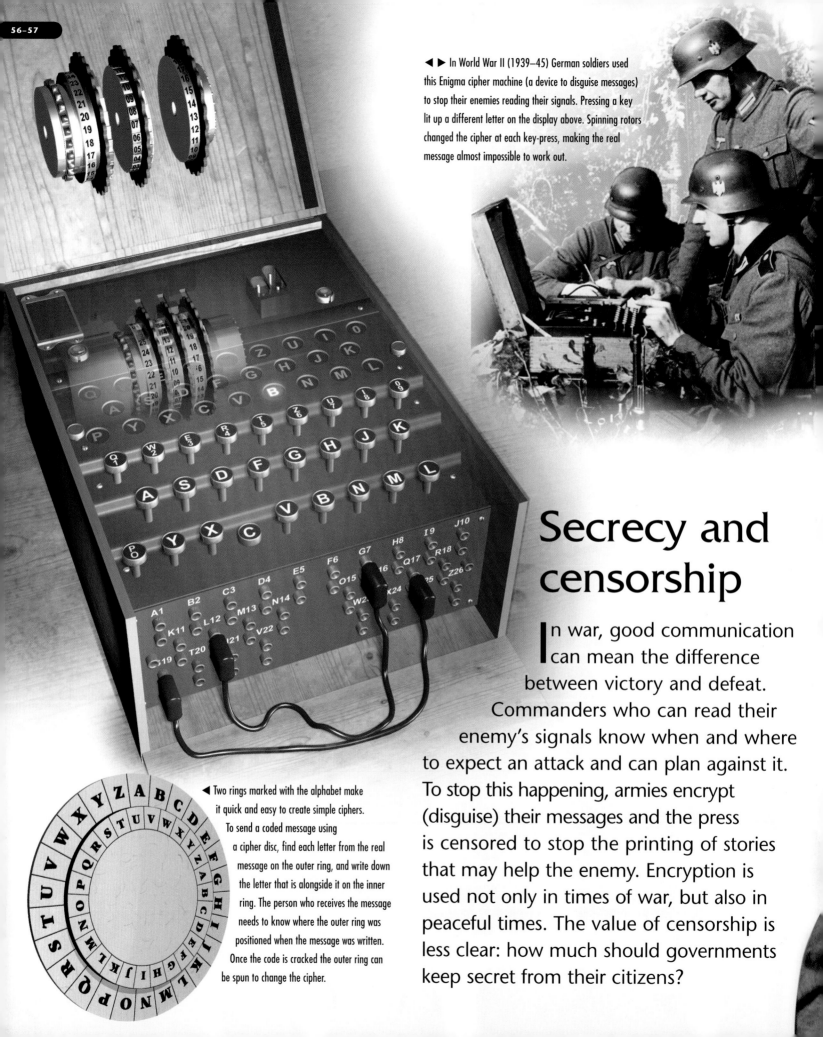

In World War II (1939–45) German soldiers used this Enigma cipher machine (a device to disguise messages) to stop their enemies reading their signals. Pressing a key lit up a different letter on the display above. Spinning rotors changed the cipher at each key-press, making the real message almost impossible to work out.

Secrecy and censorship

In war, good communication can mean the difference between victory and defeat. Commanders who can read their enemy's signals know when and where to expect an attack and can plan against it. To stop this happening, armies encrypt (disguise) their messages and the press is censored to stop the printing of stories that may help the enemy. Encryption is used not only in times of war, but also in peaceful times. The value of censorship is less clear: how much should governments keep secret from their citizens?

◄ Two rings marked with the alphabet make it quick and easy to create simple ciphers. To send a coded message using a cipher disc, find each letter from the real message on the outer ring, and write down the letter that is alongside it on the inner ring. The person who receives the message needs to know where the outer ring was positioned when the message was written. Once the code is cracked the outer ring can be spun to change the cipher.

Invisible letters

Keeping communications secret is an ancient problem. One way to do it is to make the words invisible. Messages written with a pen dipped in lemon juice or urine disappear when the paper dries. Heating the letter with an ordinary laundry iron shows up the words.

Writing in cipher

Using a cipher to encrypt the message is a more reliable way to hide it from curious eyes. To use the simplest cipher, you swap each letter for a later one in the alphabet. For example 'A' becomes 'B', 'L' turns into 'M' and 'I AM A SPY' would read 'J BN B TQZ'.

Cracking the code

Ciphers like this one are easy to unscramble if you know how they work. In English, only the words 'I' and 'A' have just one letter. So in this message, each of the two lone letters must be either 'I' or 'A'. Two-letter words are also rare, so guessing 'am' would not be too difficult.

Simple codes are so easy to crack that they are no longer used to protect sensitive information. The ciphers that scramble credit card numbers for on-line shoppers are much more advanced, and deciphering them might take years, even with the fastest desktop computers.

The need for censorship

Everyone agrees that banking details, military information and airline security methods must be kept secret. This protects a country from enemies, so governments censor news reports that reveal these details. However, it is not easy to be sure about other kinds of information. Some governments try to stop newspapers publishing stories that reveal government mistakes and corruption, or that question leaders' decisions.

▲ A padlock symbol appears on secure web pages, showing that only trusted people can read what you have keyed in.

Freedom of speech

This kind of censorship threatens the freedom of speech. Without freedom of speech, citizens cannot be sure their politicians are honest and trustworthy. For example, in 1971 the US government tried to censor the *Pentagon Papers*. These revealed facts about American involvement in the Vietnam War. After a two-week court battle, newspapers won the right to publish them.

▶ A French radio show, hosted by a DJ and a doctor, caused an uproar when controversial issues facing teenagers were openly discussed on air. Here, the hosts of the show are poking fun at their critics by pretending to be censored.

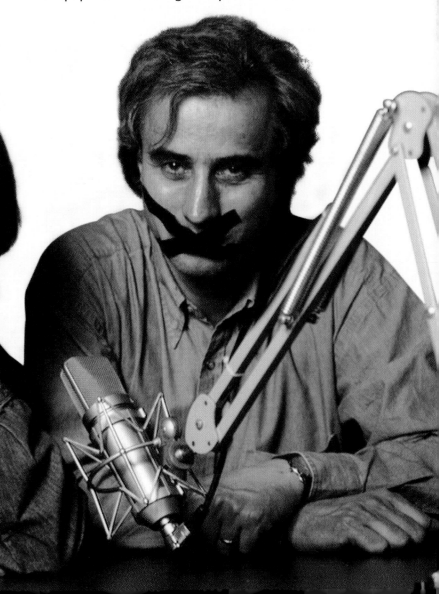

Advertising

How many advertisements do you see and hear every day? You can try keeping a total, but you will soon lose count. Most of us see up to 1,000 advertisements each day, on television, in newspapers and on the street. Even in movies, which seem to be free of commercials, advertisers pay to put famous brands in front of the camera. We cannot escape advertising – and perhaps we should not try, for it pays the cost of much of our entertainment.

A word from our sponsor...

Advertising began hundreds of years ago, when merchants painted signs to attract passers-by to their shops. In the 20th century, television and radio gave advertisers new ways to catch the attention of millions.

Today, advertising plays a vital role in keeping communications flowing. Advertisers pay to promote their products and thanks to this income, it costs us less to read publications and to receive television and radio shows. Some entertainment, such as commercial television, could not exist without advertisements. As more of us reach for the remote control during commercial breaks, advertisers have found ways to sneak their products into the plot-lines of programmes.

Cool or corrupting?

Although everyone likes getting something for nothing, advertising is not always a good thing. Commercials persuade us to buy things we do not need. They also encourage us to start harmful habits, such as smoking or over-eating. So in most countries, advertising is controlled by laws to ensure that the advertisements do not harm vulnerable people.

▲ Brands are special combinations of names, colours and shapes that make a product easy to spot on the shelf and easy to advertise. Brands stand out even when written in a different alphabet: can you identify this brand of cola?

▼ Advertising brightens up dull city views and has made places, such as New York's Times Square, famous for their bright lights. But advertising laws control where these signs appear because nobody wants to see neon reflected in a beautiful lake.

SUMMARY OF CHAPTER 4: THE GLOBAL VILLAGE

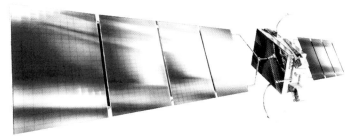

Inventing the future

Clever and imaginative science fiction writers, such as Arthur C Clarke, predicted today's wired world long before the technology to make it possible even existed. Today, we rely on satellites for countless communication tasks, including telephone calls, television broadcasts and navigation signals.

Another communications technology – the internet – began as a military command system. At one end there were radar dishes that warned of a nuclear attack, and at the other, deadly missiles that would be fired in revenge. Fortunately, the missiles were never used and the computer network that controlled them was turned to peaceful purposes. The network linked researchers and connected computers scattered around the globe.

The web's friendly face

It took special software to make the internet user-friendly. The 'world wide web' was created in the 1990s when engineer Tim Berners-Lee grew impatient with computers that could not 'talk' to each other. He invented a point-and-click interface so that anyone could find anything, anywhere on the growing network. Together, Berners-Lee's web browser and Ray Tomlinson's 1971 email invention have made the internet a popular success.

Controlling information and keeping data private on the internet are problems. However, these are hardly new challenges. Censorship is as old as news itself. Ciphers, which are used to hide credit card details on the web, began more than 2,000 years ago.

The services we use on the web seem free, but we still pay for them by viewing the advertisements that pop up on every other page. Not only does advertising pay for these web pages, but it also cuts the cost of many other broadcast and printed media. Without advertisements, we would pay a lot more for our magazines, newspapers, movies and television shows.

Go further...

 Track communication satellites: www.science.nasa.gov/realtime/jtrack

Hear the inventor of the web: www.smithsonianassociates.org/programs/berners-lee/berners-lee.asp

View a timeline of computer history: www.computerhistory.org

Advertising (Influence and Persuasion) by Clive Gifford (Heinemann, 2005)

Spy Science: 40 Secret-sleuthing, code cracking, spy-catching activities for kids by Jim Wiese (Jossey Bass, 1996)

 Advanced ink scientist Develops the inks that can be made to appear or change colour under the control of a computer.

Mathematician
Employed by national security organizations to devise secure ciphers for protecting sensitive information and to decrypt enemy ciphers.

Satellite ground station technician
Helps operate and maintain the ground equipment that sends data to and from an orbiting satellite.

Web designer
Creates web pages that aim to make online media as interesting and easy to use as their printed equivalent.

 The National Cryptologic Museum gives a glimpse into the world of codes from America's National Security Agency: Baltimore-Washington Parkway, Maryland, USA. Telephone: +1 301 688 5849 www.nsa.gov/museum

Find out how British cryptographers of World War II unravelled the 'unbreakable' Enigma cipher: Bletchley Park, Wilton Avenue, Bletchly MK3 6EB. Telephone: +44 (0) 1908 640404 www.bletchleypark.org.uk

Visit the Advertising Museum in Tokyo: www.admt.jp/en/index.html

Glossary

abroad
In another country.

amplify
To make louder.

ARPANET
A computer network set up in the 1960s by the US Department of Defense Advanced Research Projects Agency (ARPA) to allow universities to share information.

bass
The lower notes in music.

beacon
A raised structure that sends out messages such as radio signals.

broadcast
A radio or television signal that is transmitted over a wide area for many people to receive.

CAT scans
A way of building up a detailed picture of what is inside the body by passing it through a narrow beam of X-rays.

censored
Prevented from broadcasting or printing facts because they may assist a country's enemy, or embarrass leaders and powerful people.

ciphers
A method of changing messages, so that only trusted people can understand them: to others the messages look like nonsense.

culture
The things that a group of people believe, do and create, which together make them different from other groups of people.

cuneiform
A form of writing made by pressing a wedge-shaped reed into wet clay.

cutting (film or video)
The removing and rearranging of shots to make a better show.

data
The information or facts stored on a computer.

develop (a photograph)
To make visible a picture recorded on film in a camera.

digital
Made up of a long series of on-off signals, for reading by a computer.

dumb
Unable to speak.

emboss
To press a pattern into a surface.

encrypt
To encode a message using a cipher to make it unreadable to others.

etch
To burn or scratch a pattern into a surface.

exchange
A place where telephone calls are connected.

fossils
The impressions of long dead plants or animals formed when stone has replaced their tissues.

freedom of speech
The right to say what you think, even if you disagree with your country's government.

infra-red beams
The invisible rays that share some of the properties of both light and heat.

live performance
A performance for an audience broadcast or recorded from start to finish without stopping.

magnetic field
The force that exists around a magnet, and that attracts iron or steel objects.

magnetized
Made magnetic.

media
The many ways of communicating with large numbers of people, including television, radio, magazines and newspapers.

missile
A flying weapon used to attack a far-away enemy.

mixing (music)
Blending together the sound of two records so that their rhythms match.

modem
A device that converts signals into smooth waves that can travel down telephone lines.

motor neurone disease
An illness that kills the nerves that make the body's muscles move.

MP3
A way of compressing (squeezing) a digital sound recording so that it can be stored very efficiently – or a recording stored this way.

muso
A person very interested in music.

network
A group of linked communication machines such as telephones or computers.

on-line
Connected to a computer network.

operator – telephone network
A person who connects the caller to the person receiving the call.

orbiting
Circling in space.

pamphlets
Printed information that appears on a few pages loosely fixed together.

pitch
The scale of high to low sounds.

publisher
A person or company that organizes book, magazine or newspaper production and distribution.

riff
A few notes that are played over and over to provide a rhythmical backing for music.

SAGE
Semi-Automatic Ground Environment: the world's first computer network that controlled the US missile defence system in the 1950s.

scratching (DJ)
Moving a record turntable by hand to play the same section of a track over and over again.

silicon chip
A miniaturized electronic circuit that replaces thousands or millions of individual parts.

speech synthesizer
An electronic device that imitates the sound of a human voice.

spools – film
A pair of discs or frames held apart by a small tube, and used for winding up film or tape.

stammer
A speech impediment where sufferers repeat the beginning of a word.

Stone Age
A prehistoric period before people had learned to make metal tools.

treaty
An agreement, often between two or more countries.

universe
Everything in space, including the stars, the sun and earth.

web browsers
The computer software that displays pictures, text and sound, and organizes them into pages on-screen.

Index

Acknowledgements

The publisher would like to thank the following for permission to reproduce their material. Every care has been taken to trace copyright holders. However, if there have been unintentional omissions or failure to trace copyright holders, we apologize and will, if informed, endeavour to make corrections in any future edition.

Key: *b* = bottom, *c* = centre, *l* = left, *r* = right, *t* = top

Cover *l* Corbis; Cover *c* Getty; Cover *r* Getty; 1 SPL; 2 Corbis; 8*tl* Corbis; 8–9 Getty; 9*br* Corbis; 10 SPL; 11*t* SPL; 11*cr* SPL; 11*br* SPL; 12–13 Corbis; 12*tr* SPL; 12*b* SPL; 13*b* Mary Evans Picture Library (MEPL); 14*tl* Art Archive; 14*tr* Art Archive; 15*tl* Art Archive; 15*r* Art Archive; 16*tl* SPL; 17*b* Art Archive; 18*br* Corbis; 19*tr* Corbis; 19*b* British Museum; 20–21 Corbis; 20*tr* Corbis; 21*br* Corbis; 22–23 Art Archive; 22*cr* Corbis; 23*br* Alamy; 24 MEPL; 24–25 US Library of Congress; 25*bl* Corbis; 25*r* Corbis; 26–27 Corbis; 27*tl* US Library of Congress; 28 Science and Society Picture Library; 29*t* MEPL; 29*tl* Corbis; 29*br* Corbis; 31 SPL; 32*tl* Corbis; 33*r* Corbis; 34 Corbis; 35 Corbis; 36*l* Getty; 36–37*t* Corbis; 37*tr* Getty; 38*tl* Corbis; 38*cl* Corbis; 38*bl* Getty; 38–39 Getty; 40*t* Rex Features; 41*b* Corbis; 42*tl* Getty; 42*bl* Kobal; 43*br* SPL; 44–45*b* Corbis; 45*tr* SPL; 46–47 Corbis; 49 SPL; 50*bl* SPL; 51*t* SPL; 51*cr* SPL; 51*br* SPL; 52*l* Alamy; 52–53 Alamy; 53*tl* Corbis; 54 Alamy; 55*tr* Alamy; 55*bl* Corbis; 55*br* Corbis; 56*tr* Corbis; 57*b* Corbis; 58*tl* Corbis; 58 Corbis; 59 SPL; 61 Art Archive; 62 Corbis; 64 MEPL

The publisher would like to thank the following illustrators:
Chris Molan 26*tl*; Jurgen Ziewe 4*bl*; 22*t*; 23*t*; 30*tl*; 33*b*; 40*bl*; 44*tl*; 52*tl*; 58*tl*; Mike Davis 18*tl*; 29*bl*; 32*cr*; 47*br*; 58*bl*; 59*tr*

The author would like to dedicate this book to his sister, Julie.